The Great [... e

to
Tyne and Wear

by

Vernon Abbott

and

Roy Chapman

Edited by Barbara Allen

Series Editor Stan Abbott

Published by Leading Edge Press and Publishing, the Old Chapel, Burtersett, Hawes, North Yorkshire, DL8 3PB.
☎ (0969) 667566

British Library Cataloguing in Publication Data

Abbott, Vernon Ruecroft
    The Great Metro Guide to Tyne and Wear. — (RailTrail Series)
    1. Tyne and Wear (Metropolitan County) — Visitors' guide
    I. Title II. Chapman, Roy, III. Allen, Barbara, 1953- IIII. Series
    914.2870485

    ISBN 0-948135-15-8

Designer: Barbara Allen
Sketch maps: Nicholas Bagguley*
Type: Leading Edge Press & Publishing
Colour reprographics: Impression, Leeds
Printed and bound in Great Britain by Ebenezer Baylis and Son Ltd, Worcester
RailTrail series logo by Barbara Drew

*Maps are for guidance only and not necessarily to scale. For more detailed information the publisher recommends Ordnance Survey map 1:50,000, Sheet 88 and a street guide such as the Geographers' A—Z Street Atlas to Newcastle upon Tyne, Sunderland, City of Durham.

Contents

Acknowledgements

Leading Edge would like to thank Tyne and Wear Passenger Transport Executive, Gateshead Metropolitan Borough Council and Northern Arts for their help in the production of this book.

The publishers would also like to thank the following for help with photographs and illustrations:

Tyne and Wear Passenger Transport Executive
Gateshead Metropolitan Borough Council
North Tyneside Metropolitan Borough Council
Newcastle City Council
Sunderland Borough Council
South Tyneside Metropolitan Borough Council
Ian S Carr — pp16,18
John Fozard — p24(bottom)
Peter J Robinson — pp21,22,51
Side Gallery — p49
Sculpture North — pp57,58(bottom left)
Denis Ridley — p62
Stewart Bonney Agency — pp32,69,72,73
Graeme Peacock — p91
Mark Pinder — p153

FOREWORD

BY DAVID F HOWARD CBE

Director General,
Tyne and Wear Passenger Transport Executive

THESE are exciting times for the North East. The area, which has a long industrial history and which experienced rapid expansion in the industrial revolution, went through the doldrums in the 1960s and 1970s as its traditional industries declined. New and more diverse industries are coming into the area with flagship employers such as Nissan and Khomatsu capitalising on the engineering skills of Tyneside and Wearside. The economy is picking up and confidence is evident in the extent of development taking place.

Once again, we are at the forefront of progress; Gateshead's Metro Centre is the largest covered shopping area in Europe and in 1990 Gateshead hosts the National Garden Festival. This will bring many new visitors to an area steeped in history, with beautiful towns, villages and countryside and friendly, welcoming people. There are so many places to visit that good transport is essential. This is where Metro comes in.

Metro is ten years old this August and remains at the forefront of passenger transport developments. It was the first light rail system in the UK and also the first example of the conversion of underused, suburban lines to a high frequency locally owned and operated urban railway. On both counts it has continued the North East's tradition, so ably exemplified by Stephenson, Parsons and Merz, of being in the vanguard of transport initiatives, and it is signifcant that so many cities are now intent on following the pattern we set in the early 1970s, when Metro was first conceived.

Those of us who planned, built and now run Metro are conscious of our heritage. Two of the railways now incorporated in Metro — the Newcastle and North Shields, and the Brandling Junction — were 150 years old in 1989 so we painted two metrocars in their liveries to commemorate the days when rail travel was in its infancy and as such slower, not as comfortable and less reliable.

Metro trains run at least every ten minutes to the 44 stations along the north and south banks of the Tyne, providing links between the central areas of Newcastle and Gateshead, the residential and coastal resorts of Tynemouth and Whitley Bay and historical towns like Jarrow and South Shields. Local bus services linking in at many of our stations widen journey opportunities and through-tickets are available between Metro and many of them.

Metro was designed to be extended and this is now happening. The new line to Newcastle International Airport is due to open in January 1992 and studies are in hand to decide the best route to Washington and Sunderland. In the meantime, I hope you will experience and enjoy Metro as it stands. Use it to get aroud the area, there is so much to see and learn — Leading Edge's *Great Metro Guide to Tyne and Wear* encapsulates our heritage and will I am sure whet your appetite. I commend it to you and hope you will enjoy your visit and encourage your friends to experience the Great North at first hand.

March, 1990

Busways
' – reaches the parts Metro cannot reach '

☆ **Gateshead Garden Festival** — frequent shuttle from Central Station service 90

☆ **Gateshead MetroCentre** — frequent shuttle from Monument and Central Station service 100

☆ **South Tyneside Coast —Marsden and Whitburn** — from South Shields services E1, E2, X2

☆ **Stephenson's Dial Cottage Killingworth** — from Four Lane Ends services 38 and 64

The Railways of Tyne & Wear

WITHIN the lifetime of many of its people, the north east of England has witnessed phenomenal change — change which has swept away industries and ways of life which had taken centuries to develop.

The once extensive railway network has experienced much of that change, both as a victim of adverse change, of reduction and closure, and as a catalyst for improvement and progress.

From the mid-19th century through to the 1960s, Newcastle and Gateshead were the centres of a complex web of railway lines, linking the North East with the rest of the country. Striking off from, and inter-connecting, these lines were many other routes and branches — serving local collieries, towns and villages. Everywhere there was railway activity — expresses loaded with passengers, local trains carrying workers to factories and shoppers to town, goods trains transporting cargoes across the country and heavy mineral trains taking coal to the docks for shipment and carrying ore and lime to the steelworks.

Almost every factory, works and colliery had its own rail connection where traders, who would often have their own small locomotives, would busily sort the full and empty wagons.

In the past 25 years or so much of this activity has ceased. Lines, stations and sidings have closed, or been reduced to the occasional freight train. Hundreds of private sidings and works lines have disappeared — often the works themselves have closed, victims also of industrial change. Where they survive, most of their output now goes by lorry. All over Tyne and Wear you can see the monuments to a past industrial era — to history, to the railways.

All is not gloom, however, for the core of lines developed over the last century, on the whole, survives. The East Coast Main Line between London and Scotland now carries High Speed Trains at up to 125 mph (undreamt of by the builders of the railways) and is being electrified. The Newcastle to Carlisle line is still an important link across England, providing access to the beautiful wooded slopes of the Tyne Valley, while the line to Sunderland (and on to Middlesbrough) is still a useful route for passenger and freight trains.

Foremost however, is the Tyne and Wear Metro which has brought new life to the former railway lines to South Shields and the North Tyneside Loop. It has transformed a worn out, antiquated, traditional, railway network into a system which has put Tyneside to the forefront of developments in suburban rail transport in the United Kingdom — a system fit for the 21st century.

WAGONWAYS

The history of railways in the North East is inseparably linked with the history of coalmining.

As industrialisation increased during the 18th century, so too did the need for coal. The area, of course, had it in abundance — the Northumberland and Durham coalfields combined amounted to some 700 square miles contained roughly in an area bounded by Hartlepool, Shildon, Hexham and Amble — an area some 50 miles long and up to 25 miles wide.

The proximity to the coast and the rivers Tyne and Wear aided the coalfields' rapid development, for it was easy to ship coal by sea to London. It was the need to get the coal to the rivers for shipment which created the Tyneside and Wearside railway networks.

By the mid-18th century, the Tyne, below the Newcastle bridge, was thick with the ships of the coal trade, whilst between the ships bustled the Tyne keels — the boats which brought the coal from the many pits up the river. By 1910, Northumberland and Durham were producing more than 50 million tons of coal a year, of which some 19 million was exported — mostly via the Tyne to London and abroad. The association between Newcastle and coal became part of folklore, for to engage in a pointless activity was "to send coals to Newcastle".

The first railways were actually built in the coalmines themselves, where heavy weights had to be moved safely underground in confined spaces. Such "wagonways" soon extended out of the mine tunnels and down to navigable water.

The manner of the carriage is by laying rails of timber from the colliery down to the river, exactly straight and parallel, and bulky carts are made with four rowlets fitting these rails, whereby the carriage is so easy that one horse will draw down four or five chaldrons of coals, and is an immense benefit to coal merchants.

Roger Smith, 1676

The date of the earliest Tyneside wagonway isn't definitely known, but certainly wagonways were common throughout Tyneside by the 1670s. By the start of the 18th century, they had become an established way of transporting coal.

Wagonways were built on the north bank of the Tyne — from Heddon, Holywell Main, Montague, and from Wylam. On the River Wear they were concentrated on a two mile section of the river near Fatfield.

The region's largest, and most important, wagonway network was, however, on the south bank of the Tyne. Visiting the suburbs of Whickham, Blaydon, Ryton, Greenside and Chopwell today, it is hard to visualise an area peppered with small coal pits and criss-crossed with wagonways running down from shallow bell pits, open cast workings and deeper mines to the river.

Stella marked the limit of navigation of the river. Coal was transported from here and the other upper wharves downstream by keels before being transferred into sea-going colliers east of the bridge at Newcastle.

The earliest wagonways were very simply constructed from timber so little trace of them remains. However, the site of one of Tyneside's best known, was the "Tanfield" now a preserved railway, which can be visited at Sunniside.

The remains of the many small coal pits can still be traced, and can sometimes cause problems today. When the Metro tunnel under Gateshead was being dug, the sandstone was found to be honeycombed with coal measures and old abandoned workings — some dating back to the 14th century. About 20,000 cubic metres of slurry of fly ash and cement had to be pumped into the old workings to fill the many cavities!

Amongst the wealthiest mine owners of Tyneside were the Liddells of Ravensworth, who built a wagonway to carry coal from their pit at Ravensworth to Dunston Wharf. In 1726 Sir Thomas Liddell (later Lord Ravensworth), Stuart Wortley, Lord Strathmore, the Bowes family and the Montagues banded together to form a consortium known by the rather striking title "The Grand Allies". Their aim was to purchase and work collieries, and to share the cost of extending the Ravensworth wagonway, laying branches to serve collieries at Marley Hill, Causey, Tanfield Lea and South Moor.

There were some outstanding engi-

Causey Arch — the oldest railway arch in the world

neering works on the Tanfield wagon-way, the most notable being the large embankment at Breckley Burn and the Causey Arch over the Houghwell Burn. Both have survived, and can still be seen today. The embankment is 100 feet high, and 300 feet wide at the base. Built by Ralph Wood, believed to have been a local stonemason, the Causey Arch was completed in 1727, at a cost of £2,252-16s-1³/₄d! It has a span of 103 feet, its stone arch rising 35 feet from the foundations. The thickness of the arch at the centre is about 10 feet, making the 22 feet wide trackbed some 70 feet above the burn.

One of the major engineering feats of the early Industrial Revolution, and the oldest railway arch in the world, the Causey Arch was a contemporary tourist attraction. When a new route was opened to Tanfield Lea in 1820, bypassing the arch, it fell into disuse. Fortunately, it survived and is now scheduled as an Ancient Monument.

At its peak of activity the Tanfield

wagonway was one of, if not the largest carrier of coal in the country. As early as 1732 some 400 wagons were using the line each day en route to the staithes at Dunston — all of them drawn by horses. Locomotives were introduced in 1881.

The Grand Allies controlled the Tanfield for over a century until 1836 when they sold out to the Brandling Junction Railway. The new owners modernised it by converting it to standard gauge and laying iron rails. Coal was then conveyed over Brandling Junction to Gateshead, South Shields and Monkwearmouth for shipment. Eventually, the Tanfield became part of the North Eastern Railway, and then British Railways.

Today the line is a popular tourist attraction with regular passenger services during the summer. The vacated National Coal Board shed at Marley Hill is open to the public as a restored workshop and exhibition centre with 29 locomotives on show — 20 of them originally built on Tyneside.

RAILWAYS ARRIVE

By the early years of the 19th century, the complex of wagonways in Tyne and Wear began to bear some resemblance to the railway network we know today. Change was brought about by the introduction, almost simultaneously, of the locomotive and the iron edge rail on which it ran.

By the middle of the century railways were the life support system of the North East, spreading like arteries and veins throughout Tyneside and Wearside, to create one of the most complex railway networks in Great Britain. South to north ran the East Coast Main Line from London to Scotland; to the west were two lines coming together at Wylam, and running on to Carlisle; eastwards ran a line to South Shields via Jarrow and Hebburn and, from that, a line struck off along the coast to Sunderland. Northwards there was a line running parallel, and to the west of, the main line, through Jesmond to Gosforth before veering off eastwards to cross the main line to reach the coast near Monkseaton. This line then turned south through Whitley Bay, North Shields and Tynemouth to swing along the north bank of the Tyne before re-entering Newcastle. Off this line was the Riverside line which ran from Byker to Percy Main. After 1905, there was also a branch running from South Gosforth to Ponteland.

At the pulsating heart of that system was Newcastle which, by the mid-1850s, was the centre of the largest and most prosperous provincial railway company in Britain — the North Eastern Railway Company. The NER not only carried more minerals than any other railway, it also operated some of the fastest expresses in Britain, and pioneered many developments, not least the electrification of railways.

Some of the earliest NER passenger services started when miners and their families, often isolated in some valley or on bleak moorlands, were allowed to ride the mineral trains to visit the nearest market town or village for provisions or recreation. Later, a rough coach would be provided and so a branch line passenger service was born. Some of these services, solely for miners, ran until relatively recently.

In contrast, on Tyneside, as the wealthier merchants and industrialists sought cleaner air and more living space, suburbs grew up to be served by "commuter" trains. At Newcastle Central, the NER's busiest station, a flood of suburban traffic almost engulfed the longer distance travellers. At other times, the huddled masses who toiled to create the region's wealth in the shipyards, on the quays and coal staithes, in the foundries and down the mines, travelled with their families for a day out on the coast at Whitley Bay, Cullercoats or Tynemouth.

The NER was formed in July 1854, by the amalgamation of a number of other companies: the York & North Midland, the Leeds Northern, the Malton and Driffield (from August), and lastly the York, Newcastle and Berwick. Over the years it grew to have a virtual monopoly of its region — the only parallel in Britain was to be found on the Great Western Railway in south west England. The surviving lines on Tyneside are now operated either by British Rail, or the Tyne & Wear Passenger Transport Executive which runs the Metro.

BR lines — origins

The first of the above railways to carry passengers regularly — and also the first line to cross England — was the Newcastle and Carlisle. Plans for a canal between Carlisle and Newcastle had been discussed for some years, but in 1821 a study by William Chapman, of the relative merits of a canal and a railway, showed that a railway would cost about one third of the price of a canal. The Newcastle and Carlisle was announced in March 1825, and construction work began in March 1830 with the line opening in 1837. The first terminus was at Redheugh (Gateshead), from where passengers were ferried across the Tyne to Newcastle. Eventually the N&CR extended its line into Newcastle, crossing the Tyne by a bridge at Scotswood, and opening a terminus at Shot Tower in 1839. A further extension, to a temporary terminus at Forth Banks was made in 1847, and finally the N&CR ran into the new Central station in January 1851, three months after it had been opened by Queen Victoria.

The N&CR managed to remain independent when the NER was created, but it passed to the NER in 1862. The original route between Newcastle Central and Scotswood has been closed to passengers. Carlisle trains now cross the river to Gateshead and go via stations at Dunston and Gateshead Metrocentre.

The station at Wylam is one of the oldest in Britain still in regular use. But this historic village, on the wooded banks of the Tyne, has a greater claim to a place in railway history. From Wylam to Newburn, and on to Lemington Staithes, ran the Wylam wagonway, opened in 1748. The line ran a few yards from the front door of an isolated cottage called High Street House. It was here, in June 1781 that George Stephenson was born. *(See walks)*

Some years later, after the wagonway had been rebuilt from a wooden wagonway to a five-foot gauge plateway, William Hedley, Superintendent at Wylam Colliery, built two locomotives, nicknamed *Puffing Billy* and *Wylam Dilly*. (Both entered service in 1813. Modified during their long lives, the locos survived until 1862, when the Wylam line was converted into a standard gauge railway. *Dilly* now rests in the Royal Scottish Museum in Edinburgh, and *Billy* in the Science Museum in London.)

Puffing Billy

George Stephenson watched these locos at work, and seeing how they could be improved went on to build his own first locomotive at Killingworth in 1814.

Part of the route of the Wylam wagonway was used by the Scotswood, Newburn and Wylam Railway, which left the N&CR at Scotswood, to run along the north bank of the Tyne, rejoining the N&CR at Hagg Bank, just beyond Wylam. The line closed in 1968, and part of the route has been converted into an attractive landscaped walkway through the Tyneside Riverside Park. *(See walks)*

Crossing Tyneside from south to north is the East Coast Main Line, linking London with Edinburgh. The history of the building of this line is complex and steeped in the conflict and rivalry of the railway mania of the early 1840s. It is further complicated by the activities of its central character, George Hudson of York, nicknamed the "Railway King" because of his involvement in railway speculation and building. One time MP for Sunderland, Hudson was disgraced when he was found to have participated in some rather shady dealings!

A through route between London and Scotland was eventually opened in many stages. The Great North of England Railway opened its line from York to Darlington in March 1841. Northwards lay a 40-mile railway-less gap to the Tyne. The original plan was for a line direct to Gateshead, but this fell through because competition and disagreement was rife between the different railway companies who all wanted to get their hands on this lucrative stretch of line. Eventually a railway company, the Newcastle and Darlington Junction, was formed, promoted by George Hudson.

It opened a through route to Gateshead — striking north from Darlington to Ferryhill, then via Rainton Meadows to Washington, where it joined the Pontop and South Shields Railway (Stanhope and Tyne). From there the route was via the S&T to Brockley Whins, then over the Brandling Junction Railway. At last a through service between York and the Tyne was possible, and a director's special traversed the whole route for the first time on May 24, 1844. On the public opening of the Newcastle and Darlington Junction on June 18 of the same year, the first through train from London (Euston) left at 5.03am arriving at Gateshead at 2.24pm, with stops on the way totalling 70 minutes.

Such a roundabout route was inadequate, and to provide an alternative, more direct, route between Ferryhill and Gateshead, a line was opened via Durham. This is the main line of today, but its story is complicated by the fact that it was built in sections, with authorising Acts spread over the years 1823 to 1865.

Between Gateshead and Newcastle lay the obstacle of the Tyne gorge, at this point some 100 feet deep. In the year in which the railway reached Gateshead from the south, plans for the North British Railway from Edinburgh to Berwick were authorised, followed a year later by the line from Berwick to Newcastle. Robert Stephenson was engineer of the latter. He also engineered the High Level bridge across the Tyne.

In July 1847 trains had begun to run between Newcastle and Tweedmouth, departing from the Newcastle and North Shields Railway terminus in Carliol Square. The opening of the High Level bridge, however, allowed trains to run through from the south.

The bridge was formally opened by Queen Victoria on September 28, 1849. And, within a year she returned to Newcastle to open the new Central station. Started in 1847, this magnificent building was designed by John Dobson, and cost about £100,000 to build. Newcastle was the busiest station on the North Eastern Railway.

Until 1906 there were only two rail bridges across the Tyne, the Scotswood bridge for Newcastle and Carlisle trains, and, of course, the High Level which also carried road traffic on its lower deck. The three tracks of the High Level had to handle all the East Coast Main Line trains, local services to South Shields, Sunderland and Durham, and an almost continuous flow of goods and mineral trains. Congestion was worsened by the need for main line trains to reverse at Newcastle. The problem was eased when the King Edward bridge was opened in 1906. The provision of a triangular junction at the Gateshead end, together with a similar junction at the south of the High Level bridge, meant trains could join any of the other routes to the north, south, east or west.

The East Coast Main Line, as we know it today, was complete.

Metro lines — origins

NEWCASTLE AND NORTH SHIELDS RAILWAY

As Newcastle grew in the first half of the 19th century, the population spread outwards along both banks of the Tyne. To the north, this encouraged the building of the Newcastle and North Shields Railway — the world's first suburban railway designed to cater exclusively for passengers. The small terminus of the line was at Carliol Square, and the railway opened on June 18, 1839 — the anniversary of the battle of Waterloo in 1815. In honour of this, the first two locomotives were called *Wellington* and *Hotspur*, both hauling the first train from Carliol Square to North Shields, where a celebration was held.

The origins of the other lines forming the circular North Tyneside loop which comprises the bulk of today's Metro network, can be traced back some three centuries. Between 1621 and 1662, John Dove and his son were obtaining coal in the Whitley Bay area, and this was transported over a wooden wagonway to the coast at Cullercoats. In 1732, the mines were flooded, and it is believed that they were then abandoned. Further mines were sunk in the area in the early 19th century, and in 1811 a wagonway was constructed from Whitley Bay southwards to the Tyne.

BLYTH AND TYNE RAILWAY

To the north, around Blyth, the owners of the Seghill Colliery constructed various wagonways, and, to reach deeper water and enable the use of larger vessels, they decided to build a railway line southwards to Tynemouth. The Blyth and Tyne Railway was incorporated in 1852, and reached Tynemouth in 1860, using part of the course of the old Whitley wagonway. Four years later the line was extended further towards Tynemouth. On the same day (June 27, 1864) a line was opened from Monksea-ton to Newcastle, via Shiremoor. It crossed a number of wagonways, including the famous one at Killingworth, on which George Stephenson carried out many of his early experiments with locomotives. The terminus of this line was at Picton Place, where a station building was erected to the design of John Dobson, the architect of the splendid Newcastle Central station. The B&T terminus was later known as New Bridge Street.

A new line nearer the coast was authorised in 1872, but work did not start, as the NER was in the process of taking over the B&T, which it did in 1874. Work began the following year, and the new line opened on July 3, 1882. On the same day the present station at Tynemouth also opened. This superb building has survived although it is too large for late 20th century needs. Thankfully, parts of the station not needed by the Metro are being restored with substantial funding from the EC, North Tyneside Metropolitan Borough Council and PTE. These are being converted into shops and restaurants, ensuring the station maintains a valuable place in the community.

Less pretentious buildings were built at Cullercoats and Whitley Bay, although the latter was replaced by a larger building on a slightly different site in 1910.

The line was extended at the southern end under the Newcastle road to join the extended Newcastle and North Shields line. Thus, except for a few yards at New Bridge Street, there was a complete railway loop on North Tyneside, and trains ran from New Bridge Street to the coast and North Shields, then back to the Central. A link was finally built between New Bridge Street and Manors in 1909, when it became possible to travel from Central to Central in either direction, although through running did not actually start until 1917.

The Ponteland branch opened in 1905, but the line was not successful, and

Tynemouth station, built 1882 — now being refurbished

closed to passengers in 1929. Part of the branch, from South Gosforth to Kenton Bankfoot is now served by the Metro. The new airport extension — due for completion in 1991 — will use part of the remaining trackbed.

To mark the 150th anniversary of the opening of the Newcastle and North Shields Railway, Tyne and Wear Metro Car No 4051 was repainted in 1989 in a claret livery, similar to that used on some original coaches.

Much of the Metro system south of the Tyne owes its origins to the Brandling Junction and the Stanhope and Tyne Railways.

THE BRANDLING JUNCTION RAILWAY

John and Robert Brandling were lessees of coal rights in an area of South Shields. Appreciating the need for a railway to develop their business, they privately planned and promoted the Brandling Railway, to connect Gateshead, South Shields and the River Wear at Wearmouth. This later became the Brandling Junction Railway when the brothers sold

out their interests.

The first section to open was a short link from Redheugh to Hillgate Quay at Gateshead, where a connection was made with the Newcastle and Carlisle Railway. In June 1839, the line between South Shields and Wearmouth, opened followed in September by the last part of the line, from South Shields to Gateshead.

The BJR connected with the Stanhope & Tyne railway at Brockley Whins, the lines crossing each other on one level. This became known as Pontop Crossing, and was probably the first such railway crossing in Britain.

The main purpose of the BJR was to transport coal, but passenger trains also ran. Initially these were at two hour intervals on weekdays, with five trains a day on Sundays. Fares were one shilling first class, and sixpence second class from Gateshead to Wearmouth. There were four first class and 18 second class carriages.

Travel on the railway, however, was described by a contemporary as being

Brandling Junction station

"slow, dirty and rough running" while the stations were "austere and inadequate". Sometimes passengers had to travel in trains composed of coal or cattle wagons mixed with box-like coaches.

In 1842 a new station was built at Felling. It closed in 1896 when the present station opened, but still stands and can be seen from Metro and BR Sunderland line trains just south and east of Felling Metro station.

The financial returns of the BJR were initially very disappointing, probably because of poor management, rather than lack of traffic. George Hudson eventually took control of the line in 1844 as it fitted in with his plans for the Newcastle to Darlington Junction railway.

The original Wearmouth terminus of the BJR was replaced by the magnificent Monkwearmouth station in 1848 — although the Monkwearmouth Junction railway was not opened until over a year later.

In 1872, the NER opened a line off the BJR route at Pelaw, via Jarrow and Hebburn to Tyne Dock and this became the main route to South Shields and is now used by the Metro. Trains for South Shields and Sunderland thus parted at Pelaw, the former going via Jarrow and the latter continuing on the original BJR route.

The Jarrow branch was important as it served the shipbuilding and engineering works along the south bank of the Tyne and many industrial railways

connected with the line. A BR track still runs parallel to the Metro tracks to gain access to what is left of South Tyneside industry. At Tyne Dock, Metro trains rejoin part of the old Stanhope and Tyne route to South Shields.

Parts of the BJR route have, of course, closed. Most of the colliery lines have gone, as have the connections at Brockley Whins. Monkwearmouth station closed in 1967 and is now a railway museum. Yet the line occupies an important place in Tyneside's railway history and, in recognition of this fact, and to mark the 150th anniversary of its opening in September 1989, Metro car No. 4044 was repainted in the yellow livery common on BJR rolling stock.

THE STANHOPE AND TYNE RAILWAY

When the NER formed in 1854, the most important constituent was the York, Newcastle & Berwick line. Its origins go back 23 years, when the idea of a railway line from Stanhope originated with William Wallis of Westoe, South Shields. In 1831, Wallis signed an agreement to work coal at Consett and Medomsley, and limestone at Stanhope. Thus was born the Stanhope and Tyne Railroad.

Construction began in July 1832 and as little was needed in the way of cuttings or embankments (in many places the line was simply laid across the moorland), progress was rapid. The $33^3/_4$ mile length of track opened in 1834.

The S&TR built its line under the wayleave system — common in Durham and Northumberland — by which the rail company paid each landowner for the privilege of laying tracks across his land, and in most cases also paid a toll based on the amount of traffic. The traffic on the S&TR failed to reach expectations, the total expenditure on wayleaves was around £5,600, and these factors, combined with poor management, led to insolvency of the company in February 1841.

The debts incurred were the responsibility of the shareholders. One of these was Robert Stephenson, who had been consulting engineer for the line, but had accepted payment in five £100 shares rather than cash. At the end of 1841 he had to contribute the then enormous sum of £20,000 as his share of the company's debts.

To cut their losses, the shareholders decided to dissolve the Stanhope & Tyne and invest its assets in a new company, the Pontop and South Shields Railway. Under an Act of Parliament, the Pontop took over part of the S&TR. It prospered and survived to be extended and improved.

As part of British Railways, sections of the former S&TR were best known as the route of the famous iron ore trains from Tyne Dock to Consett Iron Works. The dock, with its 50-acre basin and four jetties was, until the late 19th century, the largest in the world — as well as the busiest coal shipping dock. Until 1964 two class 9 2-10-0 locomotives (the biggest on BR) worked nine-wagon trains of 500 tons of Peruvian iron ore from Tyne Dock.

Now the Consett Works have gone. Their isolation and the huge costs incurred in transporting raw materials made it uneconomical as British Steel was slimmed down for privatisation.

NCB train at Pontop crossing

On viewing the scene today, it is difficult to believe that such a major industrial complex ever existed — for little trace of the works and the railway which served it remain.

Now the only part of the former S&TR carrying frequent traffic is the length between Tyne Dock and South Shields, traversed by Metro trains.

The line between Consett and Chester-le-Street, however, forms part of a new landscaped cycleway which will eventually also reach Sunderland. The company responsible for this exciting venture, backed by Durham County Council and other authorities, is SUSTRANS — Sustainable Transport System — of Bristol. (*See page 62*)

While this imaginative scheme puts the old line to good use, it is worth considering what a passenger transport authority enjoying a wide regional remit might have done with the line which had been earmarked by the Railway Development Society as a strong candidate for reintroducing passenger trains. After all, the line could have linked the unemployment blackspot of Consett — stripped of its main employer — with Washington, home of Nissan and new industries. Regrettably, British Rail lifted the tracks with almost indecent haste after the last train ran.

ELECTRIFICATION ON TYNESIDE

The NER was one of the most progressive railways in Britain — pioneering electro-pneumatic signalling and the use of high capacity wagons. It was also a leader in electrification for railways.

Around the turn of the century, when rapid progress was being made in the development of electricity, Newcastle was a centre of expertise in this new branch of engineering. Charles Parsons applied the steam turbine to electricity generation, and the work of Joseph Swan led to the widespread introduction of the incandescent electric lamp.

During the same period, the New-castle Electric Supply Company was active in extending its distribution mains, and in 1899 Charles Merz founded the firm of consulting engineers, Merz and McLellan, which acted as adviser to the NER. Electric traction also came to the city streets — the first electric tram ran in Sunderland on August 15, 1900, and in Newcastle on December 16, 1901.

In this general atmosphere, it is understandable that the NER should become interested in railway electrification. Its chief mechanical engineer, Sir Vincent Raven, had studied electric locomotives at work in the USA and firmly believed in their benefits. The introduction of electric trams was also reducing the number of rail passengers on Tyneside quite considerably, from 9,847,000 in 1901 to 5,887,000 in 1903. As more businessmen moved to the coast and commuted daily into Newcastle, there was an obvious incentive to cater for this increased traffic and to counter the competition from the tramways.

In 1903, the NER decided to electrify the North Tyneside Loop, from Newcastle Central, via Heaton, Percy Main, Tynemouth, Whitley Bay, Monkseaton, Backworth and South Gosforth to the former B&T terminus at New Bridge Street. It was estimated that 2,844,000 passenger journeys a year originated in the area to be electrified.

The first trials of the electric trains using the "third rail" systems were carried out in September 1903, and the first passenger service started in March of the following year. The whole scheme was in operation by the end of 1904. The electric trains proved a great success, and by 1913 the number of passengers over the year had topped 10 million.

The stock built for the service was of distinctive appearance, in a striking livery of red and cream, and included three electric parcel vans, which, in the rush hours, were used to haul passenger trains composed of ordinary compartment stock, fitted with jumper cables, and with a parcel van marshalled at each end. The electric trains gave good service until August 1918 when a disastrous fire at the car sheds at Walkergate destroyed 34 vehicles and damaged many others. A mixed service of steam and electric trains was introduced, but it took nearly four years for things to return to normal.

As a result of the fire, spacious new car sheds opened at South Gosforth, adjacent to the spur joining the B&T line to the Ponteland branch. These sheds maintained the cars used on the north Tyneside services, and later became the British Railways diesel multiple unit depot. They now comprise the main depot for the Metro.

The success of the North Tyneside line led the NER to set up a committee in 1908 to consider electrifying the Newcastle, South Shields and Sunderland lines. The committee's report, completed in December that year, was in favour of electrification. In all 22 miles of double track and 10 $\frac{1}{2}$ miles of sidings were to be electrified, operated by a fleet of 84 vehicles.

Sadly this scheme was never implemented. However, in February 1935, a second committee set up by the London and North Eastern Railway (which had taken over the NER in 1923 with new national railway grouping) again investigated electrification. This time it was proposed that just the Newcastle to South Shields line be electrified and the scheme went ahead, and a 20-minute headway electric service began on March 14, 1938. The original NER designed stock was refurbished for this service while new stock for the North Tyneside lines was delivered by Metro-Cammell in 1937. In all, 128 vehicles were supplied in articulated pairs, together with four parcels vans, painted red and cream,

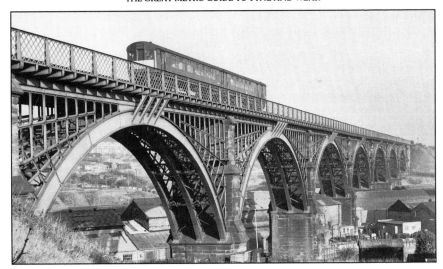

Electric train from the coast to Newcastle crosses Willington viaduct, November, 1964

recalling the original NER livery. They were repainted blue and grey in 1941.

The electric trains continued to give sterling service north and south of the Tyne for almost 30 more years. In 1960, when the rolling stock and power supply system needed renewal, BR reviewed the future of the Tyneside electric services, and it was decided to convert them to diesel multiple unit operation. BR estimated that electricity would cost £86,000 a year compared to £14,000 for diesel fuel — but that was before the 1973 oil crisis. On January 7, 1963 diesels replaced electric trains south of the Tyne. The north Tyne electric services survived until 1967, ending over 60 years faithful and reliable service. The new diesels could never match the fast electric service, as diesels could not accelerate quickly from stations.

Yet during this time, political events had been taking place which would dramatically affect the management and control of local transport. Within six years it was announced that electric traction would once again serve the region and — once again — the North

East would take the lead as innovator in rail transport.

The Metro

It wasn't just on Tyneside that BR was facing problems. By 1962, its working deficit nationally had reached £104 million. The most unprofitable passenger services were stopping trains (overall loss of £66 million), while suburban services made an overall loss of £25 million. The Commons Select Committee on Nationalised Industries in 1960 noted, with amazement and irritation, that the railways could not say exactly which of their operations were or were not losing money. The SCNI also recommended subsidisation of loss-making services retained for social reasons. This idea was not, unfortunately, adopted.

BR's financial problems led to the Transport Act of 1962 and the appointment of Dr Richard Beeching as Chairman of the British Railways Board. It was made clear that commercial principles would be paramount in the running of the railways. In terms of attempting to identify costs, and reacting to losses, Beeching's time was to be a new era for the railways. In 1963, his Reshaping of British Railways was published, advocating widespread closure of loss-making services, routes and stations, as a theoretical solution to railway deficits.

The Reshaping Report claimed that about one third of BR's existing route mileage and passenger and freight stations were losing money. An alternative rationalisation plan proposed by the unions was rejected and the next few years saw widespread service withdrawals and line closures, including a number on Tyneside and Wearside. In many cases, the "pruning of the branches" led to the withering of the "trunk" and, BR losses continued. In 1966 BR lost £134 million on operations.

The new Labour Government of 1964 seemed unhappy about the railway situation, and Dr Beeching's departure in May 1965 provided the opportunity for a fresh look. In 1967 the Government published its White Paper on the future of the railways, and the following Transport Act of 1968 introduced radical, forward looking, policies on financing and integration. Commercial viability was rejected as the prime objective of railway policy. The railway system should be designed to accord more closely with the country's needs.

At local level in some of the major cities Passenger Transport Authorities were established, comprising local councillors, charged with providing an efficient and integrated transport system, with the responsibility of deciding broad transport policy, and dealing with finance and integration of services. Passenger Transport Executives (PTEs) were professionally responsible for the implementation of the policy. Such a structure was established on Tyneside, from January 1, 1970, taking over the corporation transport undertakings in Newcastle and South Shields. In 1973 it took over Sunderland Corporation Transport, just a year before local government reorganisation led to the creation of the Metropolitan county of Tyne and Wear.

From 1972, the PTE became the major "customer" of rail passenger services — deciding on levels and quality of services, and paying the price BR quoted for providing that service. The arrangement started a process in which the county council, which became the PTA, and the PTE consulted together, each learning from the other, to develop a successful working relationship. No longer were decisions which would affect local lines made only by distant, faceless managers, but by the people who lived and worked in the region and knew its needs.

Among the responsibilities of the new county council was to decide and finance transport policies. For the first time in the history of British transport, local decision makers were to be concerned with the management of all forms of local transport, including roads, buses and rail services. BR remained responsible for day to day operation.

BUILDING THE METRO

The PTE inherited a number of problems. In 1971, only 38 per cent of households in Tyne and Wear had cars, so large numbers of people relied on public transport. Yet the rail services in the region were in decline. Trains were often shabby, stations were vandalised and it was estimated that the local rail system was losing around £1^1/$_2$ million a year. Something had to be done. The Tyne and Wear Plan Land Use Transportation Study had made an outline recommendation for a Rapid Transit System in 1971. The PTE carried out a study of the North Tyne Loop to test the strategic decisions of this earlier study in detail. It considered five alternative policies:

1. Do nothing
2. Convert the railway to a bus way.
3. Close the route.
4. Upgrade the line with new trains.
5. Convert the line to a Rapid Transit System.

The fifth option was found to be the best, giving the best overall benefits for both customers and the communities it served. In July 1973, the Tyneside Metropolitan Railway Act, giving the PTE statutory approval to build the Metro, received the Royal Assent.

Worldwide there are a large number of rail-based passenger carrying systems that cannot be called "railways", but which use railway technology. These Light Rapid Transit systems combine the best attributes of tramways — ease of access, lighter construction and high levels of safety — without the high cost of railways.

At the time, Tyneside was unique in Britain in opting for such an LRT system although at about the same time as the

Tyneside act was going through parliament, Manchester was putting forward proposals for a major upgrading of its railway system (which like Tyneside's was in need of modernisation). That proposal was for a conventional railway tunnel under the city centre — two miles long. Coupled with some improvements to the local railway lines, the package would have cost £72.6 million.

In contrast, the cost of the Tyne and Wear Metro worked out much less per mile than the Manchester scheme which in the end failed to obtain Government financial support, and was scrapped. Interestingly, the plans for Manchester have since been revived and changed, and are now for an LRT system. These have been approved and work has started. London also has its own LRT with the Docklands Light Railway.

The decision to build the Metro put Tyneside to the fore in public transport developments and demonstrated a foresight which was to bring broad benefits to the region.

The county of Tyne and Wear comprises five districts with a population of around 1.2 million. The Metro serves the four districts bordering the River Tyne. The 34-mile Metro comprises 26 miles of converted former BR lines, and eight miles of new construction, of which about half is in tunnels under Gateshead and Newcastle. As well as serving the traditional areas of population, part of the Metro serves a residential area to the north west of the city which is still developing. Plans exist for further extensions, notably the airport which should be open to passengers at the beginning of 1992.

Construction of most of the Metro was relatively simple, involving the conversion of existing rail routes. However, in the centre of both Newcastle and Gateshead substantial civil engineering was required as the Metro tunnels under the centres. It was decided that the existing railway alignments in Newcastle and Gateshead were unsuitable for conversion. Not only would there have been conflict with existing BR services, but the routes followed into the two centres were too far from the commercial cores.

At Gateshead, a major interchange was built, with a bus station at surface level, a ticket office immediately below and easy pedestrian access to nearby shopping developments. The interchange was constructed in a former quarry from which infill had to be fully excavated.

Under Newcastle there are two tunnels which cross each other roughly at right angles. The north-south tunnel is nearly one and a half miles long and the east-west tunnel just under a mile. At Gateshead slurry was pumped in to fill 14th century mine workings, while in Newcastle, ground had to be pumped

out by the Central station. Here the tunnels were driven through water-bearing boulder clay. The closeness of the Metro to the surface endangered some buildings in the city centre, and these had to be underpinned, particularly by Central station and Grey's Monument.

At Central, part of the famous portico was carefully dismantled while foundations were constructed. The two tunnels actually cross at Monument, necessitating substantial civil engineering. Shops had to underpinned and streets closed as the work was carried out.

One of the most visible parts of the Metro is the Queen Elizabeth II bridge over the Tyne. Emerging from its tunnel, the Metro strides over this impressive structure built 81 feet above the level of the river.

At Byker, the Metro runs over an impressive curving viaduct, and follows

Metro crosses Byker viaduct

Pelaw station

the alignment of a route originally reserved for an urban motorway. The viaduct is 2,649 feet long and the central piers 97 feet high.

It was the first major bridge to be built by cantilevered construction from precast concrete segments jointed by epoxy resin.

THE STATIONS

Construction of the system began in 1974 and was opened in stages, the first section from Haymarket to Tynemouth carrying its first passengers in 1980. The 26 stations on the previous BR lines were increased to 44, with new stations built at Bank Foot, Kingston Park, Fawdon, Wansbeck Road, Ilford Road, Gateshead Stadium, Bede, Chillingham Road, Hadrian Road, Smith's Park, South Shields, Palmersville and Shiremoor. Stations at Gosforth, Felling, Pelaw, Hebburn, Jarrow, Tyne Dock,

Walkergate, Wallsend, Howdon, and Percy Main replaced existing BR stations. Other BR stations have been remodelled for Metro use.

As most of the Metro stations are unmanned, easy to clean materials have been used which also give a light and attractive appearance. Public information systems are at a high level, with public address operated from the central control at Gosforth. A plentiful supply of notice boards detail how to use the system.

From the outset it was decided that general accessibility for all users, including the disabled and wheelchair bound passengers, was vital. Thus all stations have easy access from street level, with ramps, escalators or where more appropriate, lifts to platforms. At platform level, entry to the trains is made easy, as there is never more than a four inch step into the Metrocar, and the gap between the platform and the car is kept to a minimum. This policy has paid off, for nearly 250,000 journeys are made on Metro each year by disabled passengers. The major bus and Metro interchanges exist at Gateshead, Regent Centre, Four Lane Ends, and Heworth, but many other stations have good car parks to encourage park and ride.

OPERATION AND CONTROL

The Metro system consists of four colour coded routes. The yellow line runs from Pelaw into the centre of Newcastle, and then loops around the coast to terminate back at St James. The green line runs from Bank Foot to South Shields via the city centre. These two lines make up the whole of the Metro system, but there is also a red line (Pelaw to Benton via the city) and a blue line (North Shields to St James), providing a parallel service over the busiest stretches. There is a train each way on each of these lines every ten minutes, giving a weekday service at the busiest times of one train approximately every three minutes.

The Metro is controlled from a central control at South Gosforth. Nearby is the rolling stock depot and workshops where the trainmen (drivers) book on and off duty. Visit Gosforth at any time and you will witness activity. While most of Tyneside sleeps — Gosforth and the Metro is alive and busy.

The control room has three desks, each worked by one or two operators, who can keep in touch with every train, and monitor happenings at every station. Overseeing the centre is an operating supervisor.

In charge of the whole operation is the system controller who is like the old signalman, even though the Metro trains signal themselves automatically. When everything is running fine he may have little to do but monitor operations. It is

when things go wrong that he comes into his own. His knowledge is then vital, and it is at such times that he can assume the role of a signalman, to override the automatic system, setting points and signals to ensure traffic movements return quickly and safely to normal. He is also in constant contact with all drivers through radios.

Every station is connected to the control by a public address system, and all the underground stations and the interchanges also have closed circuit television. The cameras can be controlled from Gosforth and the station controller can communicate with inspectors by radio.

TICKET SYSTEMS

Originally, all ticket issue and collection was via automatic machines, and access to stations via ticket operated barriers. Reliability problems with the barriers led to them being abandoned. There are still self-service ticket machines at every station but access to platforms is now easier. To reduce fraud the Metro employs revenue control inspectors, who patrol the trains and stations regularly — and while they are primarily there to check tickets, they are also important sources of information and of general assistance to passengers.

ROLLING STOCK

The 90 articulated twin Metrocars are a British derivative of a well-established design used in Germany. Of lightweight steel construction, clad in aluminium, they have attractive, easy-to-maintain finishes. Each unit seats 84, but has a crush load of more than 200. The four access doors in each car are generously dimensioned to allow easy access by prams, pushchairs and wheelchairs.

Each train is single manned, with the trainman located in a cab at the leading end of the vehicle. Traction power is collected by pantograph at 1,500V DC.

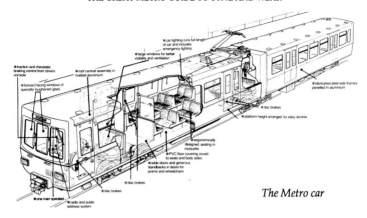

The Metro car

With good acceleration and a top speed of 50 mph, the ability to stop quickly is important. There are, therefore, three braking systems, rheostatic (when the cars' motors are connected in parallel as generators), air operated disc brakes and electromagnetic track brakes for emergency use.

THE MODERN TRAM

The introduction of the Metro brought the history of electric traction on Tyneside full circle. Many people may not realise it but a Metrocar is actually a modern-day tram, and tramway systems an early form of Light Rapid Transit. The tram's characteristic ease of access, reliability, punctuality and value for money are still golden rules for public transport today.

Unlike Britain, other countries have always valued their tramways. While planners here ripped up tramlines to make way for the bus — which in the days of cheap fuel oil were more economical to run — countries elsewhere started to modernise their tram systems. Today, there are some 300 tramways throughout the world and around half of them can be called LRTs. In 1980, Germany had 32 systems; Britain only two — the one surviving "old-fashioned" tram system at Blackpool, and, of course, the Metro.

Cities in Britain, following the Metro's lead, are now also awakening to the beauties of the modern tram. So, while the old trams may be just a memory, the ideals which made them such a success still live on.

Trams in Fulwell Road, Sunderland

THE FUTURE

Integration of bus and rail services was a central factor in the planning of the Tyneside Metro. So when the 1985 Transport Act heralded the "de-regulation" of bus services, and the separation of PTA control from the operation of former corporation bus services, it was feared that buses would operate in direct competition with the Metro. While this has happened, the reliability, frequency and value for money of Metro has meant carryings have not been substantially affected. In fact, some bus operators have voluntarily continued the integration arrangements — feeding into and out of Metro services to everybody's benefit (and especially the customer's).

Plans are already well advanced to extend the Metro two miles to Newcastle Airport, and this link should open in 1992. At present a minibus links Bank Foot Metro station with the airport — not the most satisfactory of arrangements. With the deregulation of Europe in 1992, air travel will become more important as will the role of regional airports. So it is vital that Newcastle Airport — the tenth busiest in Britain — has improved transport links.

With the decline of much of the North East's industry, new concerns have come to the region, often supported by European Community grants. A good transport system will be needed to serve this new economy properly and the Metro plans to be part of that.

The remaining BR routes in Tyne and Wear, notably that to Sunderland, are in sharp contrast to the Metro. Plans are in hand to extend the Metro to Sunderland in the 1990s and, at the time of writing, consultants were starting work on evaluating the various options, including routeing the new line via Washington. It would be very expensive to re-instate the now closed railway lines to many parts of the North East — the Metro is a more viable alternative. So as new industries come to the area, especially around Washington, Metro may link with them.

VALUE FOR MONEY?

The Metro cost some £280 million. Was it worth it? After initial criticism from some quarters, and doubts about the long term viability of the system, most, if not all, of Tyneside — from workers to employers and politicians of all parties — believe the decision to build Metro was the correct one.

Some cynics wanted the money spending on more roads. The Government, which contributed 70 per cent of the cost of building Metro, has praised it and the Department of Transport's own Transport and Road Research Laboratory has estimated that the social benefits of Metro amounted to £29.85 million in 1984/5 — more than justifying the initial costs. The ongoing benefits of Metro continue to contribute to the economy of the North East. Each year about 45 million journeys are made by Metro.

Imitation is possibly the greatest form of flattery, and such is the case with Metro. Like its forebears, the Metro has contributed to a transport revolution. As the simple wagonways of Tyneside gave birth to railways, so the Tyneside Metro has encouraged other cities to follow suit. Manchester will soon have a Light Rapid Transit system — a lighter version of the Metro — with modern cars which can actually run through city streets. And plans are being prepared for LRTs in Sheffield, Birmingham and Bristol.

By the time they appear, Tynesiders will have enjoyed the benefits of some 15 years of LRT transport.

Tyne and Wear — a short history

Tyne bridge from the south bank

Early days

Newcastle upon Tyne, the principal city of Tyne and Wear, is today the commercial, economic and cultural capital of the north east of England. Its origins however were mainly strategic.

The city started life around a bridge — *Pons Aelius* — named after the famous Roman Emperor Hadrian whose surname was Aelius. The riverside site was chosen because it presented the lowest practical bridging point at the eastern end of the Roman Wall which could also be reached by boat from the sea. It also held a commanding position, and a military camp and fort were established where the Castle Keep now stands — on the summit of a steep bank protected on either side by the ravines of the Forth and Lort Burns whose waters would have teemed into the Tyne be-

low. These ravines have now been filled in. Gateshead may also have started life around this time as it is likely that there was a fort on the south side of the river.

Despite such an impressive beginning, *Pons Aelius* wasn't an ideal place to cross the river — the site didn't become so until the erection of high level bridges in the 19th and 20th centuries. The Roman highway pattern was actually based on the Corbridge crossing some 15 miles west. Invading armies crossed at Newburn — a few miles upriver from *Pons Aelius* — where the river was fordable.

As nothing exists of the Roman bridge at Newcastle, its exact location is unknown, although it was probably near where the Swing bridge is today. It must have been an impressive structure,

26

however, as it survived long enough to establish the route which ultimately became the A1.

The Romans left the region in the 5th century. Considering the length of their stay it is surprising how little evidence, other than the Wall, remains. Much, of course, has been destroyed by centuries of subsequent development.

In the Newcastle district remains are centred on *Condercum* — the first fort west of *Pons Aelius* — in Benwell. A ruined temple and a crossing over the vallum (a ditch which ran along the south of the Wall) can be found hiding amid a housing estate on the south side of West Road in Newcastle, which follows the line of the Wall, and which bisects the site of the fort at this point.

The vallum crossing, which can be seen in Denhill Park Avenue, was created to give access to the fort from the south and its existence proves that the vallum formed the boundary ditch at a date prior to the building of the Wall and forts. Further west, at Denton Burn, the remains of a stretch of Wall, including a Wall turret, can be found adjoining the carriageway.

To see any further Roman objects in Newcastle, visit the Museum of Antiquities in the city's university.

At Wallsend, excavations on the site of the fort of *Segedunum* have revealed considerable remains of walls,

Arbeia

floors and foundations. Much of the site has since been back-filled but part of the outline is marked on the road surface near the Metro station. The Headquarters Building remains visible on the south side of Buddle Street. The actual end of the Roman Wall, which abutted the river, was removed from a shipbuilding yard and re-erected in Richardson Dees Park where it has, sadly, been subject to vandalism.

(A visit to the Heritage Centre in Station Road is recommended).

One of the best Roman relics can be found at South Shields — another Tyneside town with a substantial Roman past whose origins go back even further. The town was probably founded by the Brigantes upon a rocky promontory overlooking the Tyne estuary. It was the Romans who left their mark however. Their second century fortress of *Arbeia*, following recent clearance of overlying buildings, can now be seen almost in its entirety. The foundations and a reasonable proportion of the walls have survived local quarrying, and one of the gateways has been restored to give visitors a more vivid impression of the original structure. Other evidence can be found in the museum on the site.

From here, soldiers would have been able to see the Roman signalling station many miles south on the North Yorkshire cliffs. There is a theory that the Stanegate — the Roman road which runs south of the wall — may have continued eastwards beyond the Tyne crossing at Corbridge, presumably to Shields partly by way of the Wrekendyke Roman road from Chester-le-Street to South Shields (now Leam Lane). Boatmen from the Middle East were introduced to supply establishments further upriver.

Northumbria rules

With the downfall of the Roman Empire in Britain, the history of the Tyne and Wear area enters a very grey period. The following centuries were certainly turbulent as Picts, Scots, and invading Angles and Saxons struggled for power. By the seventh century, Britain was split into several kingdoms, Northumbria being one of the most powerful. King Edwin, who ruled from 617-633, was an exemplary Christian, and with his encouragement, preachers such as St Cuthbert played a significant part in spreading the word of the Gospel throughout his kingdom.

There have been references to a Saxon settlement at Newcastle under the name of Monkchester but there is a lack of concrete evidence for this — surprising in view of the site's central position within the Northumbrian kingdom and its place by the bridge over the Tyne. There was probably a religious settlement at Gateshead as the Venerable Bede refers to the town having an abbot called Utta.

The tremendous importance of the Northumbrian Church in Anglo-Saxon Britain is reflected in the number of churches and the standard of literature which it left behind — the *Lindisfarne Gospels* are one of its greatest legacies. Most of its churches and monasteries can be found in the countryside surrounding Tyne and Wear. In the urban area there are only two examples, although both of tremendous historical importance — St Pauls at Jarrow, founded in 681 and life-long home to the Venerable Bede, and St Peters at Monkwearmouth which contains the earliest tunnel vault in England.

In spite of the danger from seaborne attack, both are situated on waterside sites near the mouths of rivers — the latter on the north bank of the Wear and the other on the Don just before it enters the Tyne.

St Pauls and St Peters were built by St Benedict Biscop upon land given to him by King Egfrid. Much of Northumbria's reputation as a religious and cultural centre was due to the fervour and enterprise of Biscop, a well-to-do local-born churchman, who, on a journey to Italy to seek out the fount of western Christianity, brought back craftsmen and musicians to help him set up centres of learning and devotion in north east England.

Bede's *History of the English Church and People* is still in translation after 1,250 years. However — although his reputation as one of the first true historians, researching and checking his sources, is pre-eminent — other great scholars also produced some outstanding manuscripts from these monasteries including a Latin bible which is now in Florence. The bible is one of three: the fragments of a second copy were discovered recently.

The monasteries suffered badly from the Danish raids in the ninth century, as did the Royal chapel, built in the seventh century, at Tynemouth. It was not until 1090 that a monastery was refounded there — of the Black Canons under supervision from St Albans. The building, which was finished in 1110, obviously enjoyed great prestige as both English and Scottish royalty continued to visit or to be buried there.

Much of the original Norman work in Tynemouth Priory was lost in later rebuilding and extension work and the whole, with the exception of the little Percy chapel, fell into ruin. The church, which had escaped the dissolution of the Priory in 1539, was superseded in 1668 by another in the town.

Tynemouth Castle would appear to have been built to protect the Priory on its landward side, although not very successfully. Between the 11th and 17th

Tynemouth Priory

centuries it suffered many attacks and by the end of the Civil War it was in ruins. It was replaced in 1678 by Clifford's Fort on lower ground by the river. Little of this now remains, but a search around the area of the Low Lights at North Shields will reveal remains of an enclosing wall in which some of the gun ports can be distinguished.

In later times, the Castle site became a garrison fort, defended against naval attack by modern artillery. This has now been removed, along with most of the incongruous red brick barracks. Today, the Priory and Castle have the promontory more or less to themselves.

The Danes created havoc in the region but not as much as William the Conqueror and his temporary allies from Scotland who laid the countryside to waste. The Norman suppression left the North East so ravaged and depopulated that William's detailed inventory of his realm, the *Domesday Book*, did not even bother to include anywhere north of Darlington.

When, at the end of the 12th century, the Bishop had drawn up a similar record of his extensive domain, the *Boldon Book*, Wearmouth was listed as containing "22 villeins" and a handful of other households. A few other settlements such as Tunstall, which now fall within the borough of Sunderland, were of similar size. The Bishop's "town" — Bishop Wearmouth to distinguish it from Monk Wearmouth — was set upon the steep cliffs on the south side of the Wear where the river had broken through the coastal hills to form its own estuary. It never prospered and became merged with Sunderland.

The separated part of the monastery lands, across the river and east of the Bishop's land, contained a small fishing community and some think that Sunderland took its name from this "sundered possession".

Many centuries passed before the population increased above that at the time of the *Boldon Book*.

New castle

The Normans were the first to appreciate fully the strategic importance of Newcastle and, in permanent conflict with the Scots, they were not long in making full use of it. Within 15 years of invading Britain, Robert Curthose, son of William the Conqueror, built a motte and bailey castle of earth and timber on the Roman site. Thus the town got a "new castle", and, with it, a new name.

One hundred years later, in the reign of Henry II, this castle was replaced by the present Keep — a much more formidable stronghold. Except for the addition of the battlements in the 19th century — a touch of Victorian Romanticism on the part of the architect, John Dobson — the building has survived virtually unchanged and has long been an emblem of Newcastle.

The enclosing walls of the castle — the bailey — were built in the mid-13th century culminating with the erection of the barbican — now known as the Black Gate after a later owner. Before the construction of the town walls, residents of the city were dependent for refuge upon the bailey when attacked.

By the early 12th century Newcastle had become a sizeable manufacturing and trading centre and had bought out the Crown's manorial rights, establishing itself as a borough with its own officers. Soon it had a town council elected by the various trades guilds, a mayor and, by 1400, county status separate from the county of Northumberland. Most of the castle mound itself, however, remained part of Northumberland until local government reorganisation led to the creation of Tyne & Wear in 1974.

At the beginning of the 14th century, the town, including the recently incorporated suburb of Pandon, was enclosed by a wall, two miles long, seven to 10 feet wide and 14 to 25 feet high. The upper parts of the town were then still virtually unpopulated, the residents being packed into a dense mass of narrow "chares" and passages between All Saints church and the quay.

Even before the city was enclosed, four city churches had been established — St Nicholas, (raised to a cathedral in 1882), All Saints, St Andrews and St Johns. St Nicholas, erected on the site of

Castle Keep

an 11th century church, was always considered the mother church, even though the parish of the older All Saints had by far the larger population — approximately a quarter of the town's inhabitants.

With the exception of All Saints which was completely rebuilt in 1796, the churches still remain, although St Nicholas was rebuilt during the 14th and 15th centuries, and St Johns and St Andrews altered and enlarged about the same time, leaving little of the original Norman structures identifiable. Legend has it that the Scots nearly blew up St Nicholas' during the siege of Newcastle in 1644. They are believed to have decided against it after the mayor placed Scottish prisoners in the church's famous lantern tower.

31

Attempts were made at the mouth of the Tyne to establish a rival trading centre. But, even though the industrious Priors of Tynemouth were among the first to mine the shallow seams of coal nearby — subsidence into their old bell-pits still occurs — they were unable to break the monopoly on exporting which the political influence of the Newcastle merchants had secured.

Centuries later, Tynesiders were still mining coal but on a scale the Priors of Tynemouth could hardly have envisaged.

Industry arrives

From industrialisation onwards, reliance upon coal, and the heavy industries which it spawned, have monopolised the region's capital resources. This not only contributed to a lack of balance in the area's economic development, it also transformed the landscape, particularly along the banks of the Tyne and Wear.

Coal mining was first carried out, as at Tynemouth, in small drift mines or in bell pits where the coal was obtained by way of a shallow shaft until lack of lighting and ventilation made it impossible to continue further. Most of this was used locally, particularly in salt and glass manufacture. But, from Elizabethan times, it was increasingly transported in small sailing craft to London where coal burning contributed greatly to the capital's atmospheric pollution.

Several factors were responsible for the large-scale development of the industry. The building of "plateways" and, later, railways, connected distant mines to the river, opening up new coalfields. Coal was transported along these wagonways first by horse-drawn carts then by cable and gravity — in which loaded wagons going down to the river pulled the empties back up — and then by steam locomotion. Some routes used a mixture of all methods. The coal was then transferred onto "keels" and transported, by keelmen, downriver to the waiting colliers or coal ships.

Today these keelmen are no more but they have passed into Geordie folklore. They also left behind them one of Newcastle's most interesting buildings — the Keelmen's Hospital (now student flats). Built at the turn of the 18th century, this attractive two-storied dwelling was used by injured or retired keelmen and their dependents. Remarkably, the building was funded by the keelmen themselves at a cost of £20,000 out of money docked from their wages.

Most of these men lived in Sandgate by the Tyne and they figure in many Tyneside folk songs, including *The Keel Row*, *Cushie Butterfield*, *The Sandgate Lass's Lament* and *Coaly Tyne*, written in 1820:

Tyne River running rough or smooth
Makes bread for me and mine
Of all the river, north or south,
There's none like Coaly Tyne

Long has Tyne's swelling bosom borne
Great riches from the mine
All by her hardy sons uptorn—
The wealth of Coaly Tyne

Our keelmen brave, with laden keels,
Go sailing down the line
And with them load the fleet at Shields,
That sails from Coaly Tyne...

Keelmen's Hospital

Later on, the rail tracks permitted the carrying of coal to deep-water staithes, replacing the keels and thereby removing the need for extra handling, loading and unloading.

The steam engine had a wide impact on coal production, allowing the installation of pumps which were capable of pumping from far underground the water which gathered in the mine. This permitted access to low underlying seams, and made possible mining under the coastal strip of the Tyne where coal measures were overlaid by almost 200 feet of limestone.

Such expansion, however, did not come cheap. The initial costs of deep shafts, the long lead-in time before production brought any returns, and the problems met along the way — particularly where the limestone concealed the underlying coal formations — made the necessary finance more and more difficult to secure. It needed the resources of owners like the Earl of Durham to ensure such development continued.

In the 1820s the North East supplied around 95 per cent of London's coal. In 1852, the first screw-driven iron-built collier, the *John Bowes*, was launched at Jarrow. In comparison to previous coal ships, this, and its successors, could carry much larger quantities and were less dependent on weather conditions. Eventually, however, railway development elsewhere allowed other coalfields to break into the North East's near monopoly.

The growth of the coal industry continued until the mid 1920s, by which time around two thirds of the region's output was being exported to the continent and further afield.

More than a quarter of the area's working population became involved in the industry, and with that involvement came exposure to continual risk of injury and death, sometimes on an enormous scale.

A monument in Earsdon church yard commemorates 204 killed in a shaft accident at New Hartley in 1862 — a large proportion teenagers or younger.

Along the coast, salt manufacturing was the dominant industry, particularly in South Shields. It was obtained by collecting salt water from the sea and boiling it in large pans over coals until the water evaporated. The practice resulted in considerable atmospheric pollution as Daniel Defoe noted in his Tour through England and Wales in the early 18th century:

It is a prodigious quantity of coals which those salt works consume; and the fires make such a smoke that we saw it ascend in clouds over the hills, four miles before we came to Durham, which is at least sixteen miles from the place.

At the end of the 18th century coal was an invaluable asset in supplying the growing glass and paper industries, as well as a developing chemical industry, with the necessary alkalis. By mid-century Tyneside was producing 50 per cent of Britain's chemicals.

Glass-making became important in the region, particularly in Gateshead, South Shields and Sunderland. Glass itself was introduced to the area by the Saxons and there was a small industry in Newcastle in the 15th century — by 1812 there were 30 glassworks on the Tyne.

Sunderland became one of the country's leading glass-making centres due mainly to the invention here of rolled glass in 1847. However, as the century progressed, cheap imports from Belgium put strains on home production which became more and more centred on St Helen's.

The Lemington works in west Newcastle, founded in 1787, pioneered the blowing of the new electric lamp bulb but failed to keep its place in the indus-

Dunston Staithes, now restored. Coal is believed to have been carried from local pits to staithes at Dunston since the 17th century. The present structure dates from the 1890s.

try. One of Lemington's original brick cones, used to work the molten glass, still remains.

The development of the glass industry was helped by a supply of flint brought back as ballast on returning colliers. This same source enabled a large pottery industry to develop on both the Tyne and the Wear. As the 19th century drew to a close, so too, unfortunately, did the industry.

In recent years even Maling's, once the largest pottery in the country, was closed down and 200 years of commercial manufacture in the district came to an end.

Maling ware, particularly containers for tea and lids for meat and fish jars, and the decorative commemorative work produced at Sunderland, is now much in demand by collectors. Examples of local pottery and glass can be seen in museums, particularly in the Borough Road Museum at Sunderland.

Soap manufacturing was another important industry, dominated locally by two firms of which only one, Thomas Hedley, survives today under the American ownership of Procter and Gamble which rescued the ailing company just before the Second World War.

Paper-making also enjoyed a long history in the area, particularly in Sunderland where the use of esparto grass was pioneered in 1864.

Metal works

The first industry to rival the importance of coal in the area's economy was that of metal — first with the working of iron and, later, steel. Both industries became closely linked, each providing a market for the other.

By the mid-19th century, iron began to replace wood as the raw material for many products, notably wheels for the coal trucks and the rails on which they ran. There was also a large demand for anchors and chains for use on the growing fleet of colliers and, after 1850, iron plates for ships.

Iron works opened at Lemington, Walker and Jarrow between 1800 and 1842 and the lower Derwent valley was an early iron-working site of historical importance. The remains of the old Derwent Cote cementation furnace still survive to the north of the road between Rowlands Gill and Shotley Bridge, south west of Gateshead.

The most successful iron works in the district, now demolished, were at Consett where, from about 1840, the enterprise developed into the district's largest steel works and the country's leading producer of ship plates. Imports of ore, landed at Jarrow, provided much of the rail traffic between there and Consett. Plates for the Tyne shipyards passed in the other direction.

After 1880, steel replaced iron for most purposes. The older material, however, was left behind in some spectacular achievements, notably the High Level bridge over the Tyne, built in the 1840s to a design by Robert Stephenson, and the old Sunderland bridge over the Wear.

But it was another industry, and one which grew hand-in-hand with metal production, which was to dominate the fortunes of so many Tynesiders and Wearsiders during the 19th and 20th centuries. It was, of course, shipbuilding.

Ships for the world

Nowhere is this history better documented, nor with greater political impact, than in the fate of Jarrow. Here Charles Palmer set up a shipyard which had an early success with the *John Bowes*, (the first screw propelled iron collier) and 20 years later, the first tanker. To supply the Jarrow yard and another across the river, Palmer, who was already connected with the coal industry, built blast furnaces at Jarrow and Walker and acquired ore extraction rights in the Cleveland Hills. Thus he built up a huge vertical conglomerate using his own ships to carry coal to London and, on their return, pick up ore at Port Mulgrave (north of Whitby) to where the ore was delivered by rail tunnel from the mines. Discharged on the Tyne, the ore could be converted to create even more ships.

By the 1880s, production of both naval and merchant shipping was unbelievably high — shipyards on the Tyne and the Wear were still producing more than a quarter of the world's ships. But, after the slump which hit the industry at the end of the century, Palmer's fortunes fluctuated, although the 1914-18 war caused some revival.

In 1930 the National Shipbuilders Securities Company was set up to "rationalise" the industry and up and down the rivers dozens of ailing yards were bought up for dismantling and their sites "sterilised" for 40 years or more. Palmer's was the most notable victim. Unemployment in Jarrow rose to nearly 60 per cent.

The remaining yards benefitted from the revival caused by shipping losses during the second world war. On the Tyne, orders for super-tankers, which followed the closure of the Suez Canal, gave respite. Sunderland's traditional policy of mass producing standardised cargo ships also flourished until recent years, but the ending of the market for big passenger liners removed from the industry its most profitable and labour-intensive section.

With the controversial ending of shipbuilding on the Wear and the decline in merchant vessel orders on the Tyne, the river frontages are now being changed out of all recognition. Some imposing monuments remain, particularly the Sunderland piers and docks which the enterprising Wear Commissioners erected after their establishment in 1717. At a time when the merchants of Newcastle were still pocketing the dues levied on Tyne shipments, the Commissioners used their levy to create one of Britain's leading harbours. Thus encouraged, local shipbuilders were able to claim that their output exceeded that of all other British builders combined.

The creation of the Tyne Improvement Commission (now the Port of Tyne Authority) in 1850 led to similar work being carried out on the Tyne — and this was long overdue, considering the dangerous conditions at the river mouth where it was not unknown for as many as 100 colliers to be wrecked in a year.

Steam ships, of course, needed engines. Both Newcastle and Gateshead had relatively large companies manufacturing locomotives and other heavy components for railways at home and abroad.

Railway pioneer George Stephenson and his son Robert had workshops in Newcastle's Forth Street. It was here that the two built *The Rocket* and *Locomotion No 1* — the world's first passenger steam engine. Engines made by Robert Stephenson and Company were exported all over the world. The business was also involved in bridge building and other civil engineering work.

But it was Hawthorn's, also based in Forth Street, which became the giant

Below: The Stanley, shipwrecked on the Black Middens. The event led to the foundation in 1864 of the Tynemouth Volunteer Life Brigade, the first ship-to-shore rescue organisation in the country.
Right: North Shields today with the old High Light building on the left still in existence — the fish sculpture is a more recent acquirement.

in marine engine construction. Later, as Hawthorn Leslie, it was one of the world's most famous shipbuilding and engineering firms and eventually bought the Stephenson premises in Forth Street when that company moved to Darlington in 1901.

The greatest engineering works in Newcastle were those of W G Armstrong at Elswick, founded in 1847 to develop its founder's hydraulic inventions. The company's most notable achievement was the construction of the hydraulically-operated Swing bridge between 1868 and 1876. It replaced an 18th century stone bridge, built by Robert Mylne on the site of the medieval bridge which was destroyed in the Great Flood of 1771 after standing for over 500 years.

The construction of the Swing bridge, coupled with the dredging of the river upstream, opened up this section of the river to large ships. The development sounded the death knell for the keelman who consequently became redundant.

Armstrong's interest in gun design flourished during the Crimean War, and the company made use of the deepened river to build warships complete with armament for both the Royal Navy and those of other nations, Japan in particular. Much of this work was transferred downriver to Walker in 1913, although guns and, later, tanks continued to be made at Elswick.

In spite of sallies into motor car and aeroplane production the firm became completely insolvent, merging with Vicker's, of Barrow, in 1928 to become a much smaller operation.

The effect on Elswick, almost a company suburb, was devastating and countless small local investors lost their savings.

One of the most significant, and still surviving, engineering enterprises was that of Charles Parsons who developed the turbine engine. This was used in the first turbine-propelled ship, the *Turbinia*,

exhibited to great acclaim at the 1897 Spithead naval review. Parson's turbines went on to make a great contribution to the increased speed of both naval and civilian ships particularly in the transatlantic liners of the Cunard fleet in which they were installed from the end of the 19th century. One of these, the *Mauretania*, held the Blue Riband for the fastest Atlantic crossing for many years before she went to the breakers. Fortunately, the *Turbinia* did not suffer a similar fate and can be seen, fully restored, at Newcastle's Military Vehicle Museum.

Carville power station, near the centre of Wallsend, was the first power plant to instal Parson's large high speed — 2,400rpm — turbo-alternators.

Until recently, industry around Tynemouth was almost entirely confined to fishing, fish-processing and the repair and equipment of vessels, concentrated along the quay below North Shields. There remain many squares and terraces of fine houses, some converted to offices, dating from the days of maritime prosperity. The Stag Line offices overlooking the river mark the recent demise of the last of the main shipping companies; many other fine buildings at the south of the town are unfortunately neglected or derelict.

By contrast, buildings in the once prosperous area around the ferry terminus, including the Duke of Northumberland's 19th century unfinished grand approach to North Shields, have been cleaned and restored. The area has always suffered from its proximity to its more powerful neighbour — even its attempt to become the terminal of a railway from Edinburgh was doomed once the High Level bridge permitted the construction of the East Coast Main Line through Newcastle. It has also failed to maintain a position as an important shipping centre, except for Scandinavian ferry traffic.

For a variety of reasons, the large number of consumer goods industries of Tyne and Wear — tinned food stuffs, confectionery, tobacco products, health and tonic drinks, and the many products of the Co-operative Wholesale Society factories at Pelaw have now largely been lost.

The history of local industry contains many "firsts", but in surprisingly few cases was that lead maintained. Pioneering work was often not followed up and innovations, such as the electric light bulb, were developed elsewhere. Local initiatives passed into the hands of national and international companies, many of which either wound up or removed their North East operations elsewhere.

However, industrialisation left its mark. It transformed, and to a large extent, created the Tyne and Wear landscape. While environmental "improvement" schemes have disposed of many relics of the industrial period, some have been rescued. This is particularly so in the current atmosphere of preservation which recognises industrial building as an important part of our heritage.

Such a change in attitude came too late in some cases, however. The shot tower at the north end of Redheugh bridge, and the CWS mill at Newcastle Quayside goods station are examples of buildings of architectural merit or historical interest which undoubtedly would not have been demolished in today's more enlightened climate.

Towns grow

While industrialisation shaped so much of the area along the Tyne and Wear, other factors combined to create the modern townscape. Commerce, particularly, played a major role — banking has produced a number of fine buildings such as those of the Bank of England in Grey Street and Pilgrim Street, Newcastle. But the area also owes a great

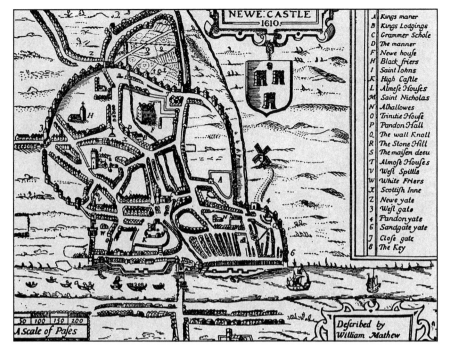

NEWE: CASTLE 1610

A	Kings maner
B	Kings Lodgings
C	Grammer Schole
D	The manner
F	Newe house
H	Black friers
I	Saint Iohns
K	High Castle
L	Almese Houses
M	Saint Nicholas
N	Alhallowes
O	Trinitie House
P	Pandon Hall
Q	The wall Knoll
R	The Stone Hill
S	The maisen deeu
T	Almost Houses
V	West Spittle
W	White FHers
X	Scottish Inne
Z	Newe yate
3	West gate
4	Pandon yate
6	Sandgate yate
7	Close gate
8	The Key

A Scale of Paßes   Defcribed by William Mathew

Newcastle in 1610.

deal to a handful of men whose vision created some of the most imposing streets and buildings to be found anywhere in the country.

During medieval times, and for many years after, most of Newcastle was undeveloped, occupied mainly by religious settlements with their gardens, orchards and pastures. The Carmelites held much of the land south of Westgate Road; the Augustinians, the easterly area where the Holy Jesus Hospital (now the Joicey Museum) stands: the Trinitarians, the upper part of Pandon; the Dominicans, the north west, where part of their Blackfriars settlement has been restored; and the Benedictines, a large site stretching from Pilgrim Street to Newgate Street, and from the town wall in Blackett Street south to High Bridge.

In 1540 this last named passed to the Crown and 40 years later to one Robert Anderson who built on it a large mansion known as the Newe House, later to be bought for redevelopment by Robert Grainger — the builder responsible for many of Newcastle's finest streets.

Before industrialisation, rich merchants lived within the densely built areas of the town near the river where their businesses prospered. Along the Newcastle Close, and even among the narrow chares off the Quayside, there were numerous mansions which looked out of place in their surroundings. The unsavoury atmosphere produced by developing manufacturing industries such as soap, however, eventually drove those who could afford it to build houses on the edge of the city centre.

As a result, few of the grand houses survived. The ill-considered auction of the Mansion House, the home of the Lord Mayor, in 1837 — which allowed the area between the Close and the river to be used for commerce — did not help.

However, there does remain an important block of timber-framed buildings at the east end of the Close, facing on to Sandhill.

Of these, the most important and accessible is the house of a banker, Aubone Surtees — father of the famous Bessie. Legend has it that she eloped in 1772 with John Scott, a coal merchant's son. Coal merchants were the life blood of the river's trade at that time and both John and his brother, as Lords Eldon and Stowell, became important political figures wielding great judicial power.

The house was rescued from decline in the 1930s to reveal the glory of its carved fireplaces and staircase. It was then turned into apartments and after that used for a variety of purposes before falling, once again, into a state of decay. Fortunately the building has now been taken over by English Heritage as its northern base (Properties in Care) and is once more open to the public.

Lord Derwentwater's town house is on the east side of the Surtees' premises. Other noblemen, such as the Duke of Northumberland, also owned town houses here as well as in London.

A few of the suburban houses, to which those whose main residence was in the Close went to escape pollution, have survived — mostly as clubs or other non-residential establishments.

Of great architectural importance are the terraces which were colonised by the emerging middle class. Although many have been destroyed, examples can still be found in most towns. They may vary in size and quality but all had a pleasant, usually unobtrusive, appearance. In Newcastle they can be seen in what remains of Eldon Square and, some of the grandest, in Leazes Terrace. More

Grey Street

modest examples are in Jesmond and off Westgate Road.

In North Tyneside they can be found in the Market Place in North Shields, and in Northumberland Square (in rather mixed condition) and Collingwood Terrace, in Tynemouth. Unfortunately, the grandest squares in North Shields — Dockwray and Toll — fell into decay and were demolished.

In South Tyneside, the satellite villages absorbed by South Shields — Westoe, Whitburn, East Boldon and Cleadon — offer the most attractive examples and the areas to the east of Fawcett Street and south of Mowbray Park in Sunderland are also worthy of note. Much has been destroyed in central Gateshead: the Saltwell area retains more.

During the Victorian and Edwardian period there was intense commercial development, particularly in Newcastle which was quickly assuming a leading role in the region. Of most significance was John Dobson's design of a unified scheme for the upper part of the city.

The project began in 1831 after Robert Grainger, a local builder who had already erected Eldon Square and several other imposing developments in the city, acquired the Newe House mansion — situated about the position of upper Grey Street. In conjunction with the Town Clerk, John Clayton, and his architect, John Dobson, Grainger was now free to carry out an ambitious scheme proposed by Dobson some years earlier.

The result was Grey Street, Grainger Street and Clayton Street together with the new interconnecting Shakespeare, Market, Hood, Nun and Nelson Streets — in effect, those parts of Newcastle which are today the pride of the city's architectural heritage.

Little credit is due to the town council which wasn't interested in Dobson's scheme. Its contribution to the townscape was the erection of new council offices and a corn exchange on the site of the old butchers' stalls between the Cloth and Groat markets, thereby blocking the view of the Cathedral spire — an action widely opposed at the time. When the old town hall was demolished just over 100 years later there was again a strong lobby to leave the space open. Unfortunately it was not successful and Newcastle acquired another office block.

When the streets were finished, they comprised a combination of business and residential premises, including the Grainger Market, the Theatre Royal (resited from Drury Lane) and the Bank of England. Clayton Street West was added in 1855, and the Central Arcade created in 1905 in the block which originally contained the Subscription Reading room and the Institution for Promoting the Fine Arts.

The focal point was the distinctive memorial column to Earl Grey (1838) situated at the junction of Grey Street and Grainger Street. With the exception of the boldly porticoed Theatre Royal, designed by Benjamin Green, and the occasional featured building such as the Bank of England with attached columns, the street façades are plain and uniform — a unity which gives a dignified look — the rising curve of Grey Street adding a stately flourish to the overall effect.

It is ironic to note that Dobson, responsible for some of the finest architecture in the city, resisted the temptation to affix his name to any of it, only later to have one of the city's ugliest streets named after him.

Commercial activities also made their mark elsewhere in the region although heavy industry still played a large part. In Sunderland, maritime concerns predominated — dock building continued in the 1850s and the Roker and South piers were constructed. One of the more attractive legacies is Monkwearmouth station, a refined classical building on a

Monkwearmouth station, Sunderland

modest scale, designed by John Dobson. It is now a railway museum. Another of the town's treasures is the water pumping station at Ryhope where the great beam engine—an immense steam-operated pump, lavishly decorated — can be seen in motion at selected times.

The erection of the North and South piers at Tynemouth and South Shields, completed in 1895, finally eliminated the hazard of the Herd Sands at the river mouth and consequently increased commercial opportunities. New docks were opened at North Shields and a fine lighthouse was erected on St Mary's island, which lies north of Whitley Bay and is joined to the mainland at low tide by a causeway. The lighthouse soon became that town's emblem.

There were also commercially-inspired developments on the south side of the river, particularly at Tyne Dock, where the huge coal staithes have now been demolished. The South Shields coast, too, received a new lighthouse at Lizard Point (though known as Souter to avoid confusion with the famous Cornish lighthouse.)

Going public

The 19th century saw the erection of many large public buildings by town councils and voluntary bodies. At the very beginning of the century, the Newcastle Guildhall, which had been rebuilt in the 17th century, was remodelled in a classical style. Later, municipal offices, varyingly impressive, arose in the local authority districts to coincide with the greatly extended duties laid upon them.

In Sunderland, municipal pride resulted in some monumental buildings, notably the Town Hall in Fawcett Street and the Library and Museum in Borough Road. None of the municipal offices built during this period can rival those at South Shields, however. The nucleus of the present building was erected in Fowler Street in 1903, including the great columned entrance with its Baroque, partially-broken pediment and the tall clock tower with its equally Baroque finial on the top.

Other public buildings of note are in Newcastle: the Central Station in its final form (1863), the GPO, St Nicholas

Street (1876); the Port of Tyne Authority, Bewick Street (1885); the Royal Victoria Infirmary main building (1900); St Nicholas Hospital, Coxlodge (1876); the old College of Medicine (now the Polytechnic Administrative block), College Street (1889); the old Armstrong College (now the centre block of the University in Queen Victoria Road)(1886-1906); the Edward VII block, head of King's Walk (1911); the old Dame Allen's School, College Road (1884); the Royal Grammar School and Central High School, Eskdale Terrace (1902); Theatre Royal and Tyne Theatre (1867) (all other major, original theatres have been demolished); Burt Hall, Northumberland Road (1885); Laing Art Gallery (1904); the Hancock Museum, (Barras Bridge).

Monuments

Most of Newcastle's main street monuments remain in their original location: Queen Victoria outside the Cathedral; Stephenson, opposite the Station Hotel; Joseph Cowan, foot of Westgate Road; The Boer War memorial, (commonly known as "The Mucky Angel") Haymarket and, most impressive of all, Grey's Monument (at the junction of Grey and Grainger Streets).

One of the region's most famous landmarks, was erected in 1844 above Penshaw village — a massive reproduction of a Greek Temple to honour the first Earl of Durham, supporter of political reform and architect of Canada's independent status.

South Shields' best known monument lies at the east end of Ocean Road, displaying a pioneer lifeboat of 1833. Across the Tyne, and impossible to overlook by anyone entering the river's estuary, is the Collingwood monument erected above the north shore in the 1840s. An immense plinth supports this impressive figure of Admiral Nelson's second-in-command at Trafalgar. In Mowbray Park in Sunderland, the monument to Sir Henry Havelock, a leading figure of the Indian Mutiny which transferred administration of India to the British Crown, still stands on top of the little hill there.

The workhouses, which form the basis of the present general hospitals, also date from the 19th century as do the infirmaries and smaller specialised institutions to care for the deaf, dumb, blind, poor and those suffering from eye or other localised complaints. Many of these buildings survive, as do some of the churches built to accommodate the movement of population from the town centres to the suburbs.

In Newcastle, work started in the 1880s on the first new buildings for the College of Medicine and the College of Science, the latter being the nucleus of the present university. About the same time, Dr J H Rutherford established a college in Bath Lane (recently demolished) for the teaching of the arts and sciences but on a less academic level. The modern college in Rye Hill is descended from this, as is the Polytechnic. A start was made around the same time on the building of public sector schools.

Due largely to recurrent cholera epidemics, extensive cemeteries had to be laid out to replace the over-used urban churchyards. Water supplies were also developed — in 1867 one eighth of all households in Newcastle were without piped water. Collection and storage of water was soon moved to the countryside, although the Exhibition Park Lake in Newcastle was an early reservoir. The series of pumping stations erected by the Sunderland and South Shield Water Company is also a great legacy of this time.

Robert Stephenson's High Level bridge, the double-decker cast iron structure with which he not only made possible the rail link to the south but also at last provided reasonably level road access to the city, still serves its purpose, as do the less adventurous King Edward rail bridge and the Ouseburn viaducts. Others built at this time have, however, been replaced, notably the famous "Chain Bridge" at Scotswood featured in the Tyneside Anthem, *The Blaydon Races:*

We flew across to the Chine bridge reet intiv Blaydon Toon
The bellman he wa callin' there — they caalled him Jacky Broon,
As saa him taakin' te sum cheps an' them he was persuadin'
te gan an' see Geordy Ridley's show in the Mechanics' Haall at Blaydon.

Bridges were built over the Wear, although the most interesting was destroyed in the 1920s to make way for the present bowstring Wearmouth bridge. This was a cast iron structure and features on a lot of local pottery. It was designed in 1793 by Thomas Paine (better known as a political philosopher than an engineer) and, unlike that over the Severn, exemplified the use of iron rather than joinery in bridge construction. It was virtually rebuilt by Stephenson in 1858 to withstand the heavier traffic it had to carry.

On the North Shields road, just beyond the old Oxford Street station, is the Master Mariners Home — a stone building in front of which stands a statue of the third Duke of Northumberland — built in 1837-40 for 32 master mariners with land provided by the Duke.

Collingwood monument, Tynemouth

Master Mariners Home, Tynemouth

The leisure age

During the Victorian age, an increase in leisure time and the financial resources with which to enjoy it, resulted in the creation of some of the area's most treasured possessions — its parks and recreational buildings. Small valleys or steep slopes were exploited — as with Mowbray Park in Sunderland, the Spital Dene in Tynemouth and Saltwell Park in Gateshead.

In Newcastle most of the denes had been filled. The Ouseburn, however, was an exception. Here a string of parks — Heaton Park, Armstrong Park, and Jesmond Dene — now provide an oasis of greenery amid the bustle of the city, and a valuable corridor for wildlife. The last two were the gift of Lord Armstrong to the city in 1880 and 1883 respectively. His landscaping of Progley Woods and other parts of the lower Ouseburn valley created an attraction of world-wide fame. He added waterfalls, bridges and buildings to the natural drama of the Ice Age gorge. One of the most notable buildings is Dobson's Banqueting Hall — now a shell, although the upper part by the renowned Victorian architect, Norman Shaw, has been preserved.

One of Newcastle's favourite recreational grounds, and one which goes back a lot further than the Victorian age, is the Town Moor. A relic of medieval times when it was granted to the town by Edward II, it represents the city's largest stretch of open space, situated just north of the city centre. Newcastle is unique among British cities to have such a prize at its heart — a vast unimproved grassland on which cows freely graze — Freemen of the city still hold the right to graze their animals there, and this right has been fiercely defended. The land is protected from development and any encroachment on its territory must be compensated for in kind.

The Moor has always been a scene of public activity — from public hangings to the more recent "Hoppings" — the largest travelling fair in Europe. Held every June, the event started life in the 19th century as a temperance festival — part of a growing campaign against the drunkenness which accompanied public gatherings. The Hoppings replaced the annual horse races which were held on the Moor for 160 years before being moved in 1882 to Gosforth Park — a venue free from grazing restrictions.

Part of the Moor was enclosed in 1878-80 to create the Bull Park, now known as the Exhibition Park. This was used for the 1887 Jubilee Exhibition and, 42 years later, for the North East Coast Exhibition. The bandstand and the domed building by the lake, now the Military Vehicles Museum, are, respectively, relics of these occasions.

One of the most popular sports during Victorian times and one which gave a further opportunity for betting, was rowing. Generations of keelmen had bred a bountiful supply of skilled and powerful oarsmen. Such was the Tyne's strength at rowing, or more specifically skiff racing (a Gateshead invention) that it could take on the rest of the world — and win. Local heroes attracted such followings that more than 100,000 people attended the funeral of the legendary Harry Clasper from Dunston — a world champion in 1845 and winner of nearly all local events. Like most local legends he is celebrated in verse:

Hadaway, Harry Lad, hadaway, Harry,
Pull like a good 'un through storm or
through shine,
Gan on, wor canny lad, hadaway, Harry!
Come to the front for the sake of auld Tyne

While the popularity of skiff racing dwindled towards the end of the last century, that of Association and Rugby Football increased. In 1892 Newcastle East End joined with Newcastle West End to become Newcastle United. A rival club at Sunderland was created with the support of local shipbuilders and mine owners.

Indoor entertainment facilities have also multiplied during the last century. The Theatre Royal, Newcastle's oldest surviving theatre — recently refurbished — was relocated from Drury Lane in the 1830s (first opened in 1778). In 1867, the Tyne Theatre was opened, its huge stage designed to take the largest London productions whose visits became possible with the introduction of fast railway services. The theatre was later turned into a cinema — the notorious, smutty Stoll — before reverting to its original use.

Other theatres in Newcastle were the Empire, the Hippodrome, the Gaiety, the Palace and the Byker Grand — all closed and demolished since the last war. Others which have been built since the war include The People's Theatre on Stephenson Road and The Playhouse and adjoining Gulbenkian Studio on Barras Bridge. All offer a wide variety of performing arts by both touring and local companies.

Of Sunderland's theatres, the Empire — erected quite late, in 1908 — has been preserved and is still in use.

The fate of many of the region's theatres was decided by the spectacular emergence of the cinema in the early part of this century. Many were converted to picture houses, including at least four in Newcastle to which were added newly-built cinemas. By the outbreak of the first world war there were 24 in the city. Many more were built between the wars, some in town centres but many in the spreading suburbs. War again marked an end to their expansion. Today the trend is towards multi-screen cinemas. The new Multiplex by Manors Metro station has nine screens. (The cinema was built on the site formerly occupied by the New Bridge Street headquarters of Metro.)

Most of Newcastle's leading city

centre hotels opened in the Victorian period. Those which survive include: The Royal Station, Neville Street; The County, Neville Street; The Crown (only the façade is now preserved), Clayton Street West; The Grand, Barras Bridge (now incorporated in the University) and the Turk's Head and Central Exchange in Grey Street (both now offices).

On the coast, Tynemouth became very successful as a tourist attraction. Fine beaches and mineral springs established it as a health resort at a very early period and it became particularly popular with literary and artistic figures. A local "school" of painters flourished rivalling those on the south coast and elsewhere. The town's popularity increased with the opening of the great winter gardens and aquarium, erected in 1878 on the sea front and followed at a later date by an open-air swimming bath. An early attempt to create a large indoor entertainment centre, The Plaza, was built on the sea shore around the same time. Although featured on souvenir pottery of the period, it achieved no great success and still awaits some successful venture.

In spite of Tynemouth's head start, the newer and brasher Whitley Bay stole the leadership of the holiday trade, its most famous man-made attraction being the Spanish City fun fair with its white dome a landmark for miles around. Tynemouth continued to present a more "refined" image.

Cullercoats Bay today

New churches

The Victorian period saw a phenomenal burst of church building due largely to a growing non-conformist congregation and the gradual migration of the population from the crowded town centres to the expanding suburbs. This building continued into the next century. Paid for by wealthy patrons, the new churches of the 1920s and 1930s rivalled those of the Victorians. After the second world war, buildings became much more modest.

Although the number of churches built during the last century are too many to mention, there are some which deserve singling out.

Pride of place must go to St George's at the head of Osborne Road in Jesmond, built in the 1880s entirely at the expense of Charles Mitchell, a shipbuilding pioneer and partner of Armstrong. Designed "in house" by Mitchell's artist son, in collaboration with his father's design draftsman, its great Venetian campanile is a landmark for miles around and can be appreciated at close quarters, thanks to the generous landscaped setting which the church enjoys. Inside there is more magnificence in the rich finishes.

Also in Jesmond, huddled by the side of a motorway access road is John Dobson's Parish church — built 20 years earlier, yet more modern in style.

Across the Ouseburn in Heaton, St Gabriels occupies a prominent site on the lip of Jesmond Vale. Its unfinished tower is another landmark; the inscription around it, viewed from one angle, causes amusement as it seems to say "Heaven and Earth are full". You must change your position to see the three words "of thy glory" which complete the dedication.

Fewer new churches were built in Sunderland than in Newcastle, yet the number was still great. Both St Columbas at the centre of Southwick and, St Ignatius in Hendon, at the opposite side of the town, are admirable buildings. The most impressive, however, is St Andrews in Roker Park Road. Built in the early years of this century, it is an immense Gothic structure of rough-hewn stone, partially concealed by trees. The influence of the Arts and Crafts Movement can be seen in its glazing and furniture.

St George's church at Cullercoats, is a very attractive building built in 1884. With its tall spire, it has long been a landmark for mariners. It is best viewed across the harbour from the old village.

Both Westoe and Harton in South Shields have attractive Victorian churches, but the best is to be found outside the suburbs in Cleadon. This delightful little church stands, with its unusual white bell housing, next to the village pond in between a Tudor house with an ancient tower and a fine mid-18th century brick house fronted with Palladian windows.

In Gateshead, St Chads on Bensham Hill is an imposing Edwardian Gothic building with an octagonal tower. Bensham also contains a Victorian church in the Norman style — St Cuthberts.

Inter-war years

Except for privately-funded churches, the inter-war years were a fairly quiet time, architecturally speaking. Financial resources were scarce and a "make-do-and-mend" philosophy prevailed. The accepted dogma was "be good to thy neighbour, and don't show off" — not a climate likely to produce any startling or impressive feats of architecture. Yet it was during this time that Tyneside gained what is now its most famous landmark — the new Tyne bridge.

The bridge, nearly a quarter of a mile long, was built during the 1920s in order to cope with the increasing level of traffic crossing the river. Opened by King George V in 1928, it soon became the symbol of Tyneside. The similar, but smaller, Monkwearmouth bridge in Sunderland was built around the same time.

New buildings worthy of note include Newcastle's Carliol House in Market Street, with its fine-looking curved exterior of Portland stone and, opposite, the Police Station, Courts and Fire Station, also in Portland stone — not a local building material but used a lot in recent years.

In Northumberland Road, the City Baths were rebuilt and a long-needed City Hall concert venue provided. In the east of the city, the University's Henderson Hall was erected, and — by the same architect, Dunbar Smith — the old library in the main quadrangle. The few new office buildings were relatively modest infill — the exception being the CWS building in Waterloo Street.

Much of the construction industry, and many small building firms, were engaged in building houses to meet the post-war shortage. There were moves towards medium-rise housing in Newcastle but probably the biggest project of this type was the Ralph Knott Memorial flats overlooking the river at Tynemouth, a dignified block in grey brick with a horizontal emphasis to match its site. It has been suggested that Hitler had the flats earmarked for a Nazi administrative HQ!

New schools were built to service the growing number of housing estates, of which the old Heaton secondary schools in Newcastle, visited by the King shortly after they opened, were the most impressive.

Other secondary schools were also constructed, such as the Ralph Gardiner at North Shields. However, given the early school-leaving age, most new building was of primary schools.

Two new industrial buildings of merit were the Rising Sun Mine at Wallsend and Dunston "B" power station in Gateshead, both now demolished.

Gateshead was also the site of the country's first industrial estate at Team Valley, built in 1936.

Tyne bridge under construction

Modern age shopping at Eldon Garden, Newcastle

Metro crossing Queen Elizabeth II bridge

Modern times

The post-war period has seen a construction boom unequalled since the days of Victorian England. Financial restraints have left their mark however, both in terms of appearance and performance—many buildings constructed during this time have already been demolished.

A clean sweep approach was much in favour. The result has had a tremendous, some would say disastrous, effect on our town centres, particularly in Newcastle where the combined effects of the Central Motorway (East) and the Eldon Centre shopping scheme have been greater than anything since the time of Grainger and Dobson.

It is too early to judge how such developments will affect the future look of the region and, indeed, how it will then be viewed — tastes change.

Certainly river crossings such as the Tyne Tunnel and the new bridges across the Tyne will be with us for a long time yet. Three bridges have been built between Gateshead and Newcastle during the last 45 years and a fourth is under construction at the time of writing.

The first of these was at Scotswood where the historic suspension bridge of 1831 was demolished, despite much protest, and replaced by a combined bowstring and box girder structure. Next came the Queen Elizabeth II bridge — commonly known as the Metro bridge — in 1981. Two years later, the old Redheugh bridge was replaced by a wider, and more attractive structure, in reinforced concrete.

The Civic Centre (1968) was a last fling of civic pride, using Portland stone — a material whose use was pioneered in Market Street between the wars. The building is most impressive on the Barras Bridge side where it escapes admirably from the tiresome "office slab" school of design. The Banqueting Hall is particularly worth a visit. The award-winning building is also notable for its use of sculpture, including the Tyne River God.

Many new buildings were added to Newcastle University, both on its established site and elsewhere in the city. They show a variety of contemporary styles — many of which now look rather dated.

In the 60s and 70s, Newcastle's Polytechnic was comprehensively developed over a large area of Pandon Dene which had been filled in during the 1880s, as well as the small terraces to the north of it and some of the richer property to the south. Among the casualties was the first recorded use of reinforced concrete in Britain — a small experimental structure made of concrete reinforced with haulage cable. Materials were Portland stone in the south giving way to brick in the north. Like the university, the style of building now looks rather dated and austere to present tastes.

Also new are the Crown Courts on the Quayside, questioniably too large in scale for their setting, and the new BBC regional TV and radio studios at Fenham, known as *The Pink Palace* to inmates.

In Gosforth, Procter and Gamble's new low-rise offices, set in a carefully landscaped area, represent an early example of a business moving out of the city into a residential area.

Elsewhere, several large factories were built while others closed — most notably Will's cigarette factory (now a listed building) on the Coast Road and Vicker's on the Scotswood river front.

A number of small local libraries were built in the Newcastle suburbs and to a high standard. Yet the new Central Library, built by the Spence partnership, is a rather disappointing building given its stable, helped in no way by its site on the newly-created, ugly John Dobson Street.

Queen Elizabeth Court on Barrack Road, was the city's first post-war high rise housing scheme but the Byker Wall is much more well-known. It makes an interesting exercise to compare the two although the former has now been revamped in a more contemporary style.

Generally, post-war public housing has been in the form of either two-storey units or blocks of flats — the success of the latter has been mixed. The Coast

Road slab blocks, well-known to viewers of *The Likely Lads* TV sit-com, have been demolished. Only a limited number of four-storey blocks have required demolition. Fortunately the Newcastle area avoided "system-built" prefabricated structures. Most private housing is of the two-storey detached variety although a number of medium size blocks have been built — mainly as sheltered units. Attractive examples can be found in the Stanhope Street area and — more upmarket — in Jesmond and Gosforth.

Futher north, the "new town" of Killingworth was created although its early high rise housing has already been demolished. The lake, however, created at the same time, is still a popular amenity and the lakeside village an interesting initiative. Also on the lakeside are the offices of British Gas whose research building sited elsewhere in the town, has been greatly praised.

In Gateshead, modern development other than housing was dwarfed by its proximity to Newcastle city centre until the arrival of the Metro Centre, that gigantic out-of-town shopping and entertainment complex. As it faces inward and is surrounded by car parks, it does not contribute much to the landscape. Many people, however, like the interior.

Gateshead has certainly come into its own in the last few years. As well as the Metro Centre, it boasts the International Stadium, now a well-known and well-used sports venue. Both have done much to raise the town's public profile — heightened even further with its selection for the 1990 National Garden Festival.

The centre of the town is not a very attractive area, due in part to the tangle of roads and railways approaching the bridges across the Tyne. However, the landscape is looking a lot better with projects such as that at Bottle Bank. *(See*

Above: Bottle Bank, Gateshead,
Top: *Killingworth Lake.* **Right:** *The Metro Centre, Gateshead.*

page 60.) Here a large-scale environmental sculpture has been created, using mostly recycled materials, between the Tyne and High Level bridges. Measuring 52 metres in length, it has been formed from rib-shaped stone piers and steel arches, built over a footpath which is an important pedestrian link to the National Garden Festival site and Riverside park. The sculpture, completed in 1986 and sponsored by Gateshead MBC Community Programme, fits in very well with the surrounding landscape and mirrors the architecture of the bridges across the river.

Other art works have since been completed as a result of the enterprising public art policy of Gateshead Metropolitan Borough council. Its on-going programme is continuing to improve the town's image and the riverside environment. Two new sculptures should appear along the south bank in 1990; another is planned for the Civic Centre, and should be finished by 1991. The new Civic Centre building itself has already helped improve the image of the town centre.

As part of its tourist development policy, the council has opened a shop called Portcullis in the Metro Centre. It contains a tourist information centre and sells high quality products from the region's craftmakers.

Of the modern architectural attractions in Sunderland, the administrative centre at Mowbray Park is particularly worth a mention. Here Basil Spence has created a complex honeycomb of spaces to give a building of modest height yet one which looks deceptively small. The subdued brickwork is perhaps not as showy as most modern buildings and its choice means it does not intrude too much on the park.

In South Tyneside the most remarkable new building is, unfortunately, a headstock for the Westoe coal mine in South Shields which is completely out of scale with its surroundings. The South Shields seafront has been developed, the Gypsy Green Stadium completed and an interesting conservation programme at Mill Dam is bringing the old riverside area back to life.

On the north side of the river there are promises — or threats depending on your point of view — of a major dockland redevelopment.

Generally, modern trends are towards greater uniformity, particularly in retailing. The rise of the shopping centre, and the continued movement towards national chains following a rash of high street take-overs, are making the main streets of our towns indistinguishable from one another, sweeping away the locally-based retailers. Older department stores like Fenwick's, Bainbridge's and Binns remain, although only the first is still a local company.

T Dan Smith, the controversial council leader behind so much of Newcastle's 60s "renewal", said he wanted to see in Newcastle city centre a 20th century equivalent of Dobson's masterpiece. Whether a development such as the Eldon Square shopping centre measures up to such a standard must remain a matter of personal judgement. Certainly, it is hard to accept the replacement of Dobson's fine Royal Arcade on Pilgrim Street as an adequate substitute. The arcade was taken down in 1963 to make way for, of all things, a roundabout.

We're making Local Travelcentres work for <u>you</u> in the Great North

P.T.E. LOCAL TRAVELCENTRES:-

BLAYDON LIBRARY
FOUR LANE ENDS METRO
HOUGHTON-LE-SPRING
(16 Mautland Square)
METROCENTRE (Bus Station)
NEWCASTLE (Central Station Metro)
NEWCASTLE (Monument Metro)
NEWCASTLE (Haymarket Metro)
SOUTH SHIELDS METRO
SUNDERLAND (Central Bus Station)
WALLSEND (High Street West)

P.T.E. Travelcentres provide:-
Local Service Guides, leaflets and tourist information. Bookings for day trips and excursions for O.K. Travel, Redby and Northumbria.
You can also buy intercity express bus tickets for National Express and Blue-Line.

You can buy a full range of tickets for Local Transport:-

For regular travellers you may find that the best ticket for you is a Network Travelticket. You can buy them for travel within a particular area or for travel throughout Tyne and Wear on Buses, Metro, Shields Ferry and the British Rail Newcastle to Sunderland Line.*

The ticket that allows you unlimited travel for a day on most bus services in Tyne and Wear, Metro, Shields Ferry and British Rail Newcastle to Sunderland Line.*

If you are making a journey outside the county an Explorer North East ticket is available covering an area bounded by Berwick in the North, Scarborough in the East, Carlisle in the West and Ripon in the South. The ticket is available for travel on bus services operated by Go-Ahead Northern, United, Weardale, Motor Services and can used on Metro and Shields Ferry*.

* - Tickets available in advance from any PTE Local Travelcentre.

If your journey involves travelling by Metro and bus you may well be able to buy a Metrolink Transfare ticket. One ticket allows you to travel by Metro and a connecting bus service.

The all day Metro ticket for travel on Metro and Shields Ferries. Available from any Metro Ticket Machine. Gives unlimited travel on Metro and Ferries on the day of issue.
Note: **Not** valid for travel on buses, British Rail services or Transfare journeys.

FOR FULL LOCAL TRAVEL DETAILS RING ...
TRAVEL-LINE (091) 2325325

TYNE AND WEAR PASSENGER TRANSPORT EXECUTIVE -PROMOTING LOCAL PUBLIC TRANSPORT

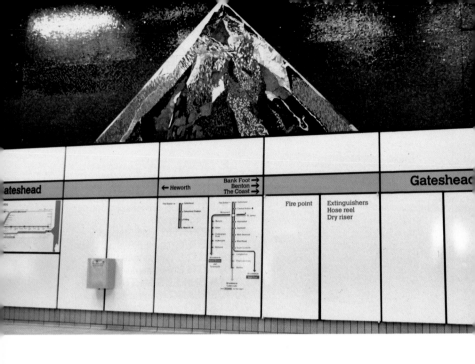

Art on the Metro

SOMETHING spectacular is happening along the highways, byways and railways of north eastern England. From stained glass windows at Monkseaton Metro station to a three and a half metre-high painted concrete sculpture in Gateshead town square, the area is alive with the largest and most extensive exhibition of public art in the country.

The transformation began back in 1977, when artist Raf Fulcher was commissioned by Northern Arts and Tyne and Wear County Council to landscape the outside of Jesmond Metro station in Newcastle. He created a series of stylised sculptures reminiscent of those triangular trees which can be found in formal gardens in the 17th and 18th centuries.

A string of works by other artists have followed as part of the *Art on the Metro* project, organised by Tyne and Wear PTE and Northern Arts and helped by funding from the Arts Council which has made monies available to local authorities in an effort to encourage art in public places.

With almost a million journeys made on the Metro every week, its stations are ideal sites for the public to experience art on their doorsteps. The idea behind *Art in the Metro* has been to provide passengers with as many different kinds of art as possible and using a variety of materials — although in some cases artists have been encouraged to work with vitreous enamels, one of the standard finishes of the Metro system.

Most of the commissions are the result of competitions in which selected artists are invited to submit their own idea for a particular station scheme. Representatives from the organising bodies (behind the project) then pick a winner.

The first work to be completed under the *Art in the Metro* title was Keith Grant's mosaic *Nocturnal Landscape*. It was commissioned to be ready for HM the Queen's official opening of the system in November 1981. The work was carried out by Gateshead Manpower Services Commission Special Programmes and followed by two further mosaics — *Night* by the same MSC team and *Day* produced at Roehampton College, London. Situated in the concourse area of the Gateshead Metro Interchange, *Nocturnal Landscape* was influenced, says Keith, by Norwegian scenery and Japanese prints.

He explains further: "The nature of my work reflects the landscape of the North East and its historical connections with Norway. I wanted a work that was calming and non-controversial both as a counter to the hurry and bustle of urban Gateshead and as an introduc-tory work to *Art in the Metro* which could become the point of departure for perhaps more challenging innovatory work in the future of the scheme."

In the first ten years of the project, 17 works were installed around the Metro network. Today, abstract murals welcome visitors to Jesmond station entrance and accompany them along the platform walls; an iron horse and carriage transports travellers back to the area's railway origins at Four Lane Ends Metro, near Killingworth; and, at Whitley Bay, youngsters on a MSC special programme have created a splendid trio of mosaics featuring a beach scene as a means to suggest the passing of time.

The importance of the *Art in the Metro* scheme is not just confined to Metro stations. From the outset the project was intended to act as a springboard for wider art practice in the North East — and it has succeeded.

Left: Night by Keith Grant at Gateshead Metro station. **Below:** *Metro Morning by Anthony Lowe at Regent Centre, Newcastle.*

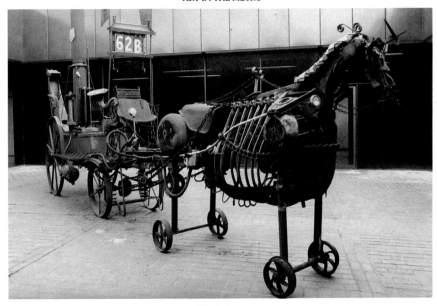

Above: Iron Horse, by David Kemp at Four Lane Ends. **Left:** *Parsons Polygon by David Hamilton at Blackett Street, Newcastle — the sculpture houses a ventilator shaft to Monument Metro station.* **Below:** *Nocturnal Landscape by Keith Grant in the concourse area at Gateshead.* **Below bottom:** *Raf Fulcher's Garden Front, outside Jesmond Metro.*

Above and inset: Stained Glass Windows by Mike Davis at Monkseaton Metro station. That on the left was the result of a Schools' Design competition, won by Rosalind Hurst. The larger, more abstract panel, designed by the artist, echoes the activities which take place on the river and coast. **Below:** Passing by Ian Patience at Whitley Bay Metro.

Public Art in Gateshead

Gateshead Libraries and Arts Service, in close collaboration with other council departments, Northern Arts and Sculpture North, is now committed to a full programme of public art throughout the Gateshead borough. In October 1986, Norman Buchan MP officially opened six major schemes. These ranged from large-scale environmental pieces to works in concrete, steel and ceramic.

Two of them — a riverside sculpture made from recycled materials at Bottle Bank, and a sculpture made from reclaimed stone taken from the old Scotswood bridge on the Tyne and sited on a disused pit heap at Windy Nook in Gateshead — have been heralded as milestones in environmental art. In both cases sculpture has been used as a means to bring back to life a landscape blighted by economic and industrial decline.

Today, there is a variety of public art work throughout the Gateshead area. The aim of all is to make the Arts available to locals — not just in galleries and museums but in places where people congregate: in the street, shopping centres and parks. Each work is individually designed for its site, most of which, fall within environmental improvement areas.

Below: Derwent Walk Express
Right: *Windy Nook*

The *Derwent Walk Express* sculpture by Andy Frost, is part of a scheme of environmental improvement at the entrance to the Derwent Walk Country Park at Swalwell. It depicts an express train travelling through a landscape setting and is in keeping with the railway heritage and historic origins of the Derwent Valley. The brightly-coloured piece is secured to the top of the viaduct abutment of the former Consett branch line.

In Gateshead's town centre, *Sports Day* by Mike Winstone, is a focal point for many shoppers. A free-standing statue in reinforced concrete, it depicts the combined themes of Aesop's hare and tortoise fable with the egg and spoon race. The idea is to represent a universal view of sport for which Gateshead is now famed.

Gateshead council was successful in securing commercial backing for this and many other works in their continuing public arts programme.

Left: Rolling Moon, sited on the riverside, by Colin Rose. *Inset*: Window, also by Colin Moon. Made of stainless steel, the sculpture, at Bensham Bank, involved a complicated series of manufacturing processes which were completed off site in locally based companies. *Below*: Sports Day by Mike Winstone

61

Lambton Earthwork by Andy Goldsworthy

Consett and Sunderland

Further south, another ambitious project will eventually incorporate a separate sculpture at one-mile intervals along the 25-mile Consett and Sunderland railway. The route is one of several constructed by Sustainable Transport Systems (otherwise known as Sustrans — a registered charity which aims to give walkers and cyclists, throughout the country, safe and attractive traffic-free paths) in partnership with Sculpture North.

The sculptures are intended to complement the environment in which they are placed and to enrich the experience of trail travellers. One is already gaining nationwide attention — the *Lambton Earthwork* by Andy Goldsworthy.

This snake-like form, winds it way for 300 metres along the route of the railway, which formerly carried iron ore to Consett steel works, and is made from materials found at the site near Chester le Street. Surprisingly, the artist claims that he didn't know of the famous local legend of the Lambton Worm when he had his initial idea for the "worm". However, he says: "Although made without the myth in mind it does give a sense of belonging, and how people relate to the work will also become a part of its nature."

Wildlife on the Metro

PASSENGERS travelling to or from Cullercoats Metro may be dismayed at the scruffy, unkempt area behind the station and along the footpath to the platform. They shouldn't be. For what looks like a dumping ground to human eyes is actually a haven for many birds which feed and nest in the Hawthorn, Elder and Bramble growing there.

Cullercoats is typical of many railway sites which provide a valuable habitat for many of our native species — a survey carried out in 1989 by Northumberland Ecological Services for the PTE identified a large variety of wildlife and vegetation surviving in and around Metro stations and along the tracksides.

A triangle of land between the Palmersville Metro and the nearby main line BR station, for instance, is a wildlife haven, sheltering many types of plants which in turn provide cover and food for birds and mammals. The soil, like that around most railways, is not very fertile. Fortunately, however, there are a surprisingly large amount of species which prefer things this way.

At Palmersville, these include Common Toadflax and Oxford Ragwort both of which have adapted to survive in well-drained areas and in poor soil conditions. Grasses include Common Bent and Creeping Bent, Black Knapweed, Vetches and Bird's Foot Trefoil — all of which give a welcome home for invertebrates, frogs, newts and small mammals. Many species of tree have been planted and these provide suitable nest sites and food for birds. Some of the trees also support invertebrates. The wooded area will increase in wildlife value as the trees mature.

At Tynemouth, 62 species of birds have been recorded from the station area where mature trees provide good cover particularly for commoner birds such as Thrush, Blackbird and Pied Wagtail. The number includes several rare species, and it would appear that migrant birds reaching the north east coast are using the Tynemouth corridor to move inland. Berried shrubs along the tracksides are also a good source of food for winter migrants such as Fieldfares and Redwings which migrate to Britain from Scandinavia.

The NES survey established the value of the Metro System as a series of "green corridors" which pass through land often inhospitable to wildlife. The policy of the PTE to limit use of herbicides along the track means that these areas support a larger variety of plants than other systems such as roadside verges. Lack of human disturbance and pollution also enhance their value to wildlife.

The survey also produced recommendations about how the trackside could be maintained to satisfy the operational needs of the Metro system while protecting and enhancing the wildlife value of the land. This will lead, in the future, to a detailed management plan which will identify those areas of the system which should be managed and how. The PTE's long-term aim is to promote the Metro as the most environmentally-friendly way to travel.

Fieldfare

Pied Wagtail

Tyne and Wear Metro

Route Map

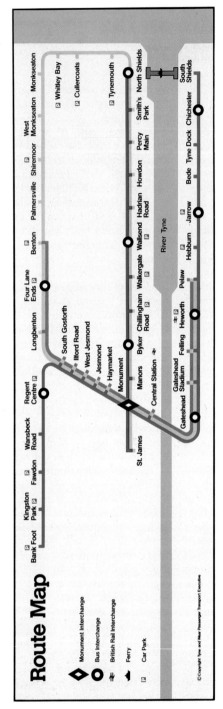

Stations shown: Bank Foot, Kingston Park, Fawdon, Wansbeck Road, Regent Centre, Longbenton, Four Lane Ends, Benton, Palmersville, Shiremoor, West Monkseaton, Monkseaton, Whitley Bay, Cullercoats, Tynemouth, South Gosforth, Ilford Road, West Jesmond, Jesmond, Haymarket, Monument, St. James, Manors, Byker, Chillingham Road, Walkergate, Wallsend, Hadrian Road, Howdon, Percy Main, Smith's Park, North Shields, South Shields, Central Station, Gateshead, Gateshead Stadium, Felling, Heworth, Pelaw, Hebburn, Jarrow, Bede, Tyne Dock, Chichester

River Tyne

Legend
◆ Monument Interchange
○ Bus Interchange
⇌ British Rail Interchange
⚓ Ferry
🅿 Car Park

©Copyright Tyne and Wear Passenger Transport Executive

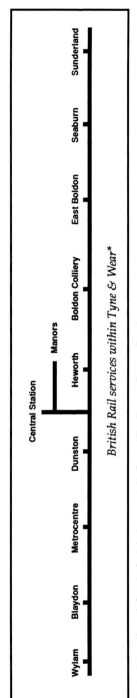

Central Station

| Wylam | Blaydon | Metrocentre | Dunston | | Heworth | Manors | | | East Boldon | Seaburn | Sunderland |

British Rail services within Tyne & Wear*

*Services between Newcastle Central to Sunderland are supported by Tyne and Wear Passenger Transport Executive

64

TOWN TRAILS

Newcastle :

Newcastle:
lower city and riverside

3 miles
This walk takes in some of the city's oldest buildings and
most interesting landmarks — including the old town walls,
Castle Keep, Cathedral, and Tyne bridges.

AFTER admiring the interior of the main line Central station turn right along Neville Street, leaving through the main portico. This fine building, designed by John Dobson, was opened by Queen Victoria in 1850 and the portico added in 1863. The entrance to the Metro is near the site of the Hospital of St Mary the Virgin. This has now disappeared except for one of its gate piers now repositioned at the corner of the new building adjacent to the Stephenson monument opposite.

The Royal Grammar School, founded in the 16th century and formerly located in the Cathedral churchyard, took over the hospital premises in 1600 and remained there until the building was demolished in 1844. Dobson saved two of its columns which were re-erected at the present school in Eskdale Terrace, Jesmond, as part of the school's fourth centenary celebrations.

On the other side of the road is a statue of George Stephenson by local sculptor, John Lough, and erected in 1862. On the south side of the road are the Royal Station Hotel, built at the same time as the Central station, the Bolbec Hall (1909) and Neville Hall (1870). The last two have long associations with the mining, shipbuilding and engineering industries. Between them is the Literary and Philosophical Society, now nearing its bicentenary.

Cross the lower part of Westgate Road as it swings right towards the castle and pass along Collingwood Street. This,

with its continuation Mosley Street, contains several imposing banks built last century. Lloyds, on the right, is a pleasant example and more restrained than some others. Mosley Street was the first British street to be lit by gas, and, later, electricity.

At the next junction, opposite you, is the Cathedral, previously the parish church of St Nicholas and raised to its present status in 1882. *(See page 30/31)* Its most distinctive feature is the remarkable 15th century, 193 feet high, lantern tower borne on diagonal arches — thought by many to be the most beautiful of its kind. The original church of 1091 was burned in 1216. The present building evolved after that date with the probable exception of the crypt. In the south transept is an interesting memorial to Henry Maddison, a 17th century public figure, which incorporates over 20 members of his family.

Leave by the north door. In front of you is a monument to Queen Victoria. The modern building behind it, between the Groat and Cloth Markets, stands on what must have been an excellent spot from which to view the Cathedral steeple before other buildings got in the way — first butchers' stalls, then the old Town Hall and Corn Exchange, demolished in the 70s to make way for an office block.

Turn left round the Tower to face the General Post Office (1876), and continue round to your left to Milburn House at Amen Corner. On this brick turn-of-the-century office block, facing the cathe-

Newcastle from the South bank with the distinctive lantern tower of St Nicholas Cathedral and the Castle Keep dominating the scene

dral, you will find a tribute to Thomas Bewick whose wood-carving workshop was on that site. The steep street running down the side of the culverted Lort valley is the Side. Lord Collingwood was born in one of the houses which were demolished when Milburn House was built, as recorded above a doorway. This steep narrow street was once the main road between bridge and town. Beyond it on the Castle knoll is the Black Gate, in the 17th century the home of

Patrick Black but originally the Castle barbican. The lower portions, including the archway with its provision for portcullis and drawbridge are 13th century.

As you pass through it you will notice an excavated gap — once a narrow street of shops — between it and the railway which was constructed through the middle of the Castle bailey. Under the railway arch and into the Garth on your right is the Castle Keep.

This substantial building with walls

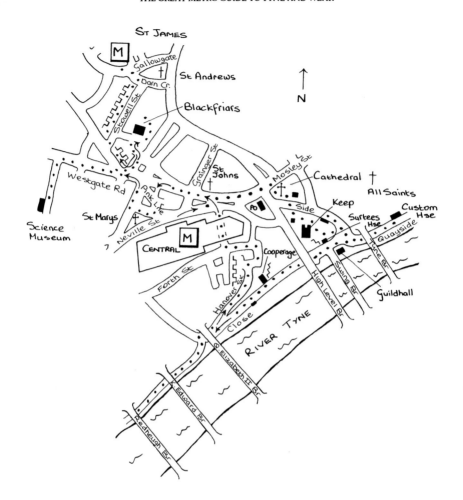

up to 18 feet thick, a massive square tower and angle turrets, is undoubtedly the most impressive military building in the area, and one of the finest square Norman keeps in the country.

Access is by an external staircase leading to an upper floor containing the great hall. Note the restored decorated Norman arch at the main entrance. There is also an attractive Norman chapel at a lower level beneath the entrance.

The Keep was part of a royal castle built at the command of Henry II in the 12th century and which replaced Curt-hose's wooden "New Castle" of the previous century.*(See page 30)* It was built by the same person who designed and built King Henry's mighty keep at Dover Castle and remained in royal ownership until last century. The roof and battlements are 19th century additions.

The climb to the roof is worth the effort to see the excellent views of the lower parts of the city and the great, though now diminished, railway intersection below, once said to be the world's largest diamond crossing.

The Castle bailey came under the control of the sheriff of Northumberland on behalf of the Crown and, until 1974, it was, as the "rural district of Newcastle", part of the County of Northumberland. The building on the east side is the old County Hall built on county territory, though the far end, added in 1933, extended over the boundary and attracted city rates. Opposite it is the Moot Hall, a pleasant Greek revival replacement (1812) of the Great Hall in the Castle bailey in which the Sessions were held. From the far side there is a view down to the rear of Elizabethan mansions on the Close. To the right of the Moot Hall is the South Postern and a short stretch of bailey wall.

Make your way down from the Postern to the Close. There are few buildings left alongside the Castle stairs, once a clog-making area. Turn left along the Close, which prior to the industrial era, was the most fashionable place to live, colonised by rich merchants and country noblemen when they were in town. A few houses still survive, such as those belonging to Aubone Surtees and Lord Derwentwater. *(See page 40)* The former is now the northern headquarters of English Heritage and is open at the usual hours. It contains a fine Elizabethan staircase and fireplace. It is best known as the house from which Surtees' daughter, Bessie, eloped in 1772 with Jack Scott, son of a coal exporter who lived by the Sandgate. Soon reconciled with his banker father-in-law, Jack Scott prospered and became

Lord Eldon, who with his brother, Lord Stowell, held the two most powerful political positions in the country.

Turn the corner into the Side. The view is dominated by an immense arch carrying the main railway line north, beyond it the right fork is Dean Street created by the culverting of the Lort Burn in the 1780s. In one of the old warehouses on your left is the Side Gallery devoted mainly to photographic exhibitions — many of international standing — and film shows.

Cross the street and continue eastwards under the Tyne bridge, the north abutment with one of the pivots of the bow can be seen on your left. Note the imposing office blocks of the departed shipping merchants, some of which are now residential. Look up King Street for a fine view of All Saints Church.

Just beyond King Street is the Custom House, a dignified and classical

Bessie Surtees House

building originally built in 1766 although remodelled in the 19th century. Note the royal coat-of-arms above the door. Newcastle used to have the only customs house on the river and fought to keep things that way as it helped the city maintain control of riverborne trade. Eventually, however, customs houses were built at North and South Shields.

If making this tour on a Sunday morning visit the famous outdoor market which takes place along the full length of the Quayside, otherwise turn here, for a view of the first of the river bridges, opened in 1928 by King George V. This provided a direct four-lane link for the Great North Road from Gateshead High Street to Barras Bridge by way of Pilgrim and Northumberland Streets. As you pass back under it, the Guildhall is in front of you, guarding the entrance into the Close.

The Guildhall, traditionally the centre of power in Newcastle, was erected in the 1650s, although much of what can be seen today is the result of a series of alterations and enlargements made following riots in 1740 and a fire 50 years later. The rioters, many of them keelmen, were provoked by corn merchants who withheld cheap grain supplied to them to relieve hunger after a bitter winter and spring had created a food shortage.

Most of the work took place between 1796 and 1826 when the building's exterior was converted from a Gothic to a Classical style. It contains several fine rooms and carved finishes including the magnificent 17th century timber-roofed guildroom. From this side of the Close is the best view of the timbered houses opposite.

Beyond the Guildhall is the second bridge and the traditional bridging site from Hadrian's time onwards. The medieval bridge — which used to be lined with houses — was destroyed in 1771 and replaced by a nine-arched stone structure. This still effectively set an upper limit of navigation to ships however. It wasn't until Armstrong's hydraulic Swing bridge replaced it in 1876, largely to permit the development of his Elswick shipyards, that shipping could pass further upriver.

The third bridge is the High Level — a cast-iron double decked structure erected in 1849 by Robert Stephenson. Its lower deck gave the first level road route from Gateshead to the centre of Newcastle. The bridge belonged to the railway which charged pedestrians a toll of a halfpenny whether they crossed by horse-drawn bus or by foot. The journey cost a whole penny by tram!

Passing westwards along the Close you come to Arthur's Cooperage — a timbered building at the foot of yet another stepped passageway, the Tuthill Stairs, leading from the river to the upper city. Now a pub, it survived as a working cooperage until recently. Between the Close and the river at this point stood a fine 17th century mansion house with a quay for the Mayor's decorated barge; unfortunately it was burnt in 1895.

Continuing past the site of the Close Gate you pass under the steel Queen Elizabeth II bridge which carries the Metro over the Tyne. This was the first part of the urban riverside to be touched by industry — a development which eventually drove rich inhabitants out of the Close.

Past Forth Banks, Skinner Burn Road continues the road westwards under the fifth crossing — the King Edward railway bridge. This carries the main line direct from the Team Valley into the west end of Newcastle's Central station, bypassing Gateshead West station. The bridge was opened in 1906, and is a fairly utilitarian metal structure on stone piers.

The sixth and newest bridge is the Redheugh. Made from reinforced concrete, it replaced a narrow, weak, metal bridge built in 1871. One of its functions is to carry water and gas mains across the river. The new bridge is an elegant structure which, viewed from below, belies its four-lane width.

There used to be a leadworks shot tower at the north end of Redheugh bridge but this unfortunately has been demolished.

There is a space of almost three miles before the next group of bridges at Scotswood — the gap was once navigated by four ferries.

The return walk can be made via Forth Banks and up Hanover Street past fine old warehouses. At the top is Hanover Square — once a select residential area and one with several historical associations. Early schools were established here by the Church of the Divine Unity and the Hospital for Sick Children first opened here.

The hospital lay just within the town walls and a tour of these is best started in Orchard Street just round to the west — the removal of a brewery has opened up part of the stretch between the Neville and White Friars Towers. Behind the builders' merchants opposite were the engineering works of Robert Stephenson. Some of these can still be seen. From Orchard Street a tunnel under the Central station leads you back to Westgate Road.

Having crossed the roads near Stephenson's Monument, turn left up Westgate Road. On your right is one of the old city churches, St Johns. Although a building in decorated and perpendicular styles of the 14th and 15th centuries, it dates back at least to Edward I and contains masonry from an earlier Norman structure.

Across Grainger Street is the original Savings Bank, beyond it, the Courts, and finally, the Old Assembly Rooms. The latter were constructed in the grounds of St John's vicarage between 1774 and 1776 to the design of William Newton, and were once known as the New Assembly Rooms to distinguish them from predecessors in the Groat Market. Fortunately the fine interior with two rooms almost 100 feet long, has been preserved for its original use, whereas its successors, the New Assembly Rooms at Barras Bridge, are now the University sports department.

Opposite the Assembly Rooms, across Fenkle Street is a monument to Joseph Cowan, a newspaper owner and radical politician — he is reputed to have smuggled arms and red shirts (red for freedom) to Garibaldi's guerrillas. The iron-shaped building on your right at the intersection of Westgate Road and Fenkle Street was the scene of the disastrous Cross House fire which led to fire precaution legislation.

Cross Westgate Road to the narrow entry leading to Pink Lane. On your right are buildings which are being restored to house arts-related projects. Pink Lane is part of the road which ran along the inside of the town wall which together with the Gunner and Pink Towers and the Forth Gate between them, have disappeared.

Cross Pink Lane and Bewick Street to St Mary's RC Cathedral, built in 1844 to a design by Pugin. The fine 260 foot spire was added around 1870. On the opposite side of Clayton Street there used to be a large hotel, now shops and apartments. On the right, Pink Lane continues to the site of the West Gate. Just up Westgate Road, on the left is the Tyne Theatre, rescued from destruction when it became a cinema in 1919.

In the 1880s and 90s it was the meeting place of the Sunday Lecture Society which brought many international figures to Newcastle — including Gladstone in 1891.

The theatre has now reverted to its original use and boasts an exceptionally large stage which has retained the

Blackfriars

complex machinery needed to mount theatrical spectaculars.

A short distance up Westgate Hill, Blandford Street leads to the Science and Engineering Museum.

Crossing back to the north side of Westgate Road turn up Cross Street, just below the traffic lights, crossing Charlotte Square to Blackfriars — a Dominican friary founded in the 13th century. Only the foundations of the chapel remain but buildings round the cloister, which survived the Dissolution as meeting places for various guilds, have been restored. These include craft workshops, an information centre with a visual presentation of local history, and a pleasant restaurant. More of this Dominican Friary remains than of any of the other religious houses which occupied so much of the town. It was here that Edward Baliol took his oath of fealty to Edward III and where Percy and Douglas fought before the Battle of Otterburn. The fight occurred by the town wall. (The Friary's gate in the wall

had to be built up in times of siege and can still be identified.) At the Dissolution it was the largest of the friaries and in 1544 the corporation bought it from the Crown for leasing to the guilds. Beyond the Friary is what is now called "Chinatown" with many restaurants and shops stocking Chinese delicacies. Phone boxes have been given a "pagoda" look by British Telecom.

Return to the traffic lights at the site of the West Gate and follow the western walls. Since the demolition of Dr Rutherford's College opened by the future George V in 1894, and of the School of Science and Art opened 15 years earlier by the Marquis of Hartington, the outer face of most of this stretch of wall is visible. The inner face, however, is probably more interesting and accessible. A walk along it will take you past the surviving Durham, Heber, Morden and Ever Towers to the gap made by the street traditionally known as Darn Crook. To your left and across Gallowgate is St James Metro.

Newcastle: the markets & northern city

2½ miles

*Some of Newcastle's more recent architecture is visited on this walk
through the newer parts of the city. These include the Eldon Square
shopping centre, university, polytechnic and Civic Centre.*

Civic Centre

FROM the Monument Metro station leave the pedestrian area by Grainger Street, with Boots on your right. At one time the garden of Anderson Place occupied this part of the town. The present streetscape is the result of the celebrated 19th century scheme of Grainger, Dobson and Clayton which was implemented inside the north wall which ran along the line of Blackett Street. *(See page 41)*

Turn right into Nelson Street; the alleyways on your left lead into the Grainger or Butcher Market. Many of the shops are still butchers, though practically every line of trade is represented, including Marks and Spencer's Penny Bazaar, the forerunner of their larger establishments. Weaving your way through the gridiron of alleys to the right, you enter the more open part of the market which is spanned by a glass roof. Here the trade is mainly in fruit, vegetables and flowers. Walk across and

73

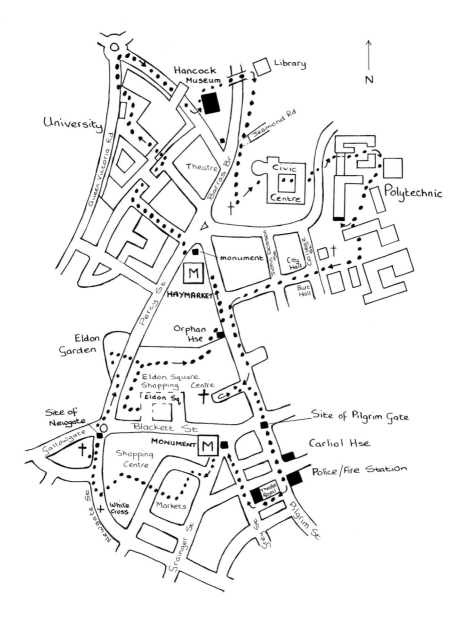

enter Clayton Street. The far side is mostly new —the exception is a bow-fronted pub — and forms part of the Eldon Square shopping centre.

Enter the new fruit market and take the escalator to the upper floor. Veer left to leave by the escalator down to Newgate Street. On your left, at the widest part of the street, is a mark in the road which indicates where the White Cross stood and where a livestock market was held. Beyond it Low Friar Street leads to Blackfriars. To your right is St Andrew's church, occupying the north-west corner of the walled town; part of the wall can be seen in the churchyard. The Norman chancel and nave arches proclaim the church's age, but there have been many alterations since then, particularly following damage by Scottish cannon fire in 1644.

Leave the church and turn left to the roundabout marking the site of the New Gate, which was not only a fortress but also a debtors' prison. Cross the foot of Gallowgate to Barclays Bank and continue along Percy Street, one of the first suburbs outside the walls. The narrow street on your left leads to Leazes Park and the Moors which once stretched down to the town walls. Enter the Eldon Garden, take the elevator and cross back to the Eldon Square Centre. Turn right as far as Blackett Bridge, but instead of crossing it, exit left to Old Eldon Square. Only the east side of the Georgian square now remains, but it helps to give an indication of what the original would have looked like. In the square stands the city war memorial.

Retrace your steps through the shopping centre, turn right at the junction and proceed to Northumberland Street. Turn left to the circular concourse of the Haymarket Metro station and the "Mucky Angel" which is actually a South African War Memorial. The statue was dismantled when the Metro station was under construction as it was thought vibrations from the building work might damage it.

Turn left and cross Percy Street at the traffic lights. Enter the university precinct opposite the memorial; the tall building on your left with a slate-faced lecture theatre projecting from the far end is the Physics Department. Most of the new buildings were designed by architects associated with the School of Architecture, though this one is actually by Basil Spence. Beyond it lies the Department of Agriculture and the 1939 red-brick School of Medicine, now rehoused beyond the nearby infirmary. In front is the Department of Chemistry.

Turn right and pass under the Union debating chamber. Pause at the junction with King's Walk. To the right is Barras Bridge and St Thomas' Church, flanked on the left by the Playhouse and Gulbenkian Theatre and on the right by the original pre-war Union building, the new Assembly Rooms and the Grand Hotel building, both part of the University,

Turn left through the double arch (1911) to find the Museum of Antiquities on your left and the Hatton Gallery to your right. The museum contains mainly Roman relics, including a reconstruction of a Mithraic temple, while the gallery houses both temporary exhibits and a permanent collection, including a work by Kurt Schwitters.

Schwitters, a Dadaist painter, was a refugee from Hitler's Germany in the 30s and stayed for a time in the Lake District. He was particularly fond of creating constructions using bits of rubbish — creating art from non-art. One of these — a Lakeland bothy wall which he covered with a variety of objects, but left unfinished when he died in 1948, was transported to Newcastle in the 60s.

Passing through the quadrangle, you will find on your left Armstrong College (1888-1906). It had started life in

1871 as the College of Physical Science next to the School of Medicine in Westgate Road, but later took the name of the famous engineering magnate. In the 1930s it merged with the College of Medicine to become Kings College under the University of Durham. This formed the nucleus of Newcastle University, established in 1963.

On the right is the School of Architecture and the old library. Facing Queen Victoria Road and the Royal Victoria Infirmary is the Percy Building, which houses Greek antiquities. Pass to the right of the building on to the road, then turn right to the roundabout. Turn right again, to pass between the Electrical Engineering (right) and the Mechanical and Civil Engineering buildings. After going under the Geography building, the Hancock Museum is on the left.

The museum was built by the Natural History Society, mainly to house a collection of birds assembled by the Hancock brothers. However the spacious galleries (open daily) also contain more general displays, including some impressive fossils. At the side of the museum, by the pavement, is a reconstructed burial chamber. In front of it, facing Barras Bridge, is a monument to Lord Armstrong.

Retrace your steps past the side of the museum and turn to the right, leading to a covered bridge over what used to be the Great North Road. This takes you to the new Library. Turn down the footway next to the road to leave the University, cutting across Jesmond Road, a pleasant terraced street now freed from through traffic.

Continue by the roadside to the Gothic church of St Thomas the Martyr; there are memorials either side of the west entrance. The church was built in 1830 by John Dobson. It is not actually a parish church, being built to replace a 13th century chapel at the end of the Tyne bridge. The chaplain used to be the keeper of the bridge and with the Dissolution the chaplaincy remained an appointment of the Mayor and Corporation.

In 1611 a royal charter attached the chapel to the Hospital of St Mary Magdalene, at Barras Bridge, which also had passed to the corporation so a connection with this part of the town had been established by the time the bridge chapel was demolished in 1830.

Cross the wooded area on the left of the church to the Civic Centre. To the left is the "drum" of the Council Chamber and beyond it the Banqueting Hall; in front of you are the Committee Rooms. Before passing under them note the River God Tyne sculpture on the wall to your left and, next to it, an engraved glass screen. To your right, gas-fired flambeaux line the ceremonial road. Across the vaulted undercroft is a decorative wrought-iron portcullis which can be raised and illuminated from below.

During working hours you will be able to enter the central court. Two sides of the lawn have a linear fish pond lined with fountains; down the nearest side a jet plays upon a flock of bronze geese "taking off" from the water. On your left is the Wren Stone, which bears the mark of approval of that famous architect when selecting stone for St Pauls Cathedral and London churches.

Within the entrance next to it is an information desk where you may be able to arrange a tour of the inside of the building.

Leave the court by the glass doors at the far end of the terrace; when the building is closed, make your way round by the access roads at either end onto Sandyford Road.

You will come out opposite the Polytechnic Arts building, Fashion Centre — which enjoys a reputation as a national leader in its field — and Library. Go under the Arts building to the left of the pedestrian crossing, and bear left to the Humanities building. Turn right, and beyond the building on your right, turn in that direction; on your left are halls of residence. Beyond the second building on your right, bear right diagonally across a court, with the Students' Union on your left. At the far corner is the entrance to the Polytechnic Gallery, which holds various exhibitions, mainly contemporary, including work by the Norwegian artist, Munch.

From the gallery turn left along the terrace; pass under the building and across a court to Northumberland Road. The building opposite, constructed around another court, houses the Science and Engineering departments. The Presbyterian church to its right is now incorporated into the Polytechnic, the congregation having joined that of St James' church opposite — cruciform in plan and with a tall central spire. Next to it are the former premises of Dame Allan's School. This is a pleasant small building and like the church dates from the 1880s. Opposite, on your left, is a large brick building. This used to be the College of Medicine before it was incorporated into Kings College in the 1930s and now houses the Polytechnic administration.

Cross College Street to the City Hall and Baths, built in 1928 on the site of older baths. Opposite is Burt Hall, erected in 1895 by the Northumberland Miners' Association as a tribute to their leader, the first miner MP. Separated from it by a drill hall is the new TGWU office. Cross the dual carriageway of John Dobson Street and continue along Northumberland Road to the semi-pedestrianised Northumberland Street — unrecognisable as the old A1 of a few years ago. Turn left.

Notice the light-coloured building (Saxone shoe shop at time of writing) on the right which carries statues of local worthies — John Marley, Thomas Bewick, Harry Hotspur and Roger Thornton.

This was the site of an "Orphan House", built by John Wesley in 1742. It was the second of his chapels in the country — the first one was at Bristol three years earlier — and one of the city's earliest schools.

At the far end of Fenwick's store turn right into Brunswick Place. At the end of it is Brunswick Methodist church, built in 1821 to replace the Orphan House. The church exterior is original but the interior has recently been remodelled with a floor at balcony level.

Go back to Northumberland Street then cross Blackett Street on your right. You are now back in the area of the old walled town. Continue down Pilgrim Street. At its junction with Market Street are two major buildings from the interwar years — one home to the Police and Fire Stations and the other Carliol House with its gently curving facade. Both are made of Portland stone, a material which was used quite a lot in the area in the years immediately following the last war, but rarely before these examples. Brick has now returned to favour.

Take the next turn right into Shakespeare Street, and then turn right again into Grey Street to Monument passing the Theatre Royal on your right. This has been recently refurbished with more spacious staircases and bars as well as better backstage facilities. This was its second major alteration this century. The exterior remains the same as Benjamin Green designed it in the 1830s to replace William Newton's theatre in Drury Lane, off Mosley Street.

An entertaining scene in the centre of Newcastle, dominated by the towering monument to Earl Grey.

Newcastle: the east city

1¹/₂ miles

*A short but fascinating trail around the
eastern end of the city centre including
the old suburb of Pandon.*

FROM the Monument Metro station walk to the foot of Grey's Monument itself and take advantage of the fine city views down Grainger Street and the gently curving slope of Grey Street with its theatre, banks and offices. Grainger Street runs down to the Central station and is predominantly a shopping street.

To the west Blackett Street is taken up with the Eldon Centre, the 1930s "Dutch modern" Fenwick building, with its horizontal bands of wide-jointed brickwork, and the art nouveau Emerson building dramatically reflected in the mirror glass of the Eldon Centre. The Blackett bridge in the distance completes the view.

Eastwards along Blackett Street, the architecture is mixed. It is richest on the south side, and much of the north side is being rebuilt. Beyond Northumberland Street and Pilgrim Street, (the old A1), the Pearl Assurance building has been rebuilt in an uncompromising 1960s style — it used to have an old advertising sign with flashing light-bulbs.

The monument is a 133 foot high Greek column surmounted by a statue of Earl Grey of Howick, built in 1838 to commemorate the passing of the 1832 Reform Act under his leadership. You can, on Saturdays, climb the winding stairs up to the platform below the statue to enjoy a panoramic view of the city. Of the buildings around the pedestrian area, the Central Arcade is an interesting 1905 insertion after a fire, into the facade of an older building by Grainger. The walls are terracotta below a glass vault and the mosaic floor has recently been restored.

On the opposite side of Grey Street is the Lloyds Bank building, housing a bookshop and the Eldon Grill. These have survived from the last century virtually unchanged. Between these premises an inscription proclaims one of the first purpose-built cinemas. This area was the site of Anderson Place and, before it, the Franciscan Friary.

Walking east and crossing the head of Pilgrim Street (the site of the Pilgrim's Gate), notice the modern building beyond the Pearl — the public library. Past the "subterranean" John Dobson Street is the Laing Art Gallery (closed Mondays) looking somewhat "out on a limb" since the removal of the old library to the left of its tower. The gallery was given to the city in 1904 and most of the items in the collection come from private donations. A large number have local connections.

At this point, in front of the Laing, stood the Carliol Tower at the north-east corner of the town, where the wall turned south along Croft Street. Beyond Higham Place a dance-hall incorporates John Dobson's own house: not a great tribute to the town's best-known architect; nor is the street named after him. Opposite is another building that is faring rather better. Recently vacated by the BBC, the old Lying-in hospital is now being restored. The hospital was built in 1826 to a design by John Dobson

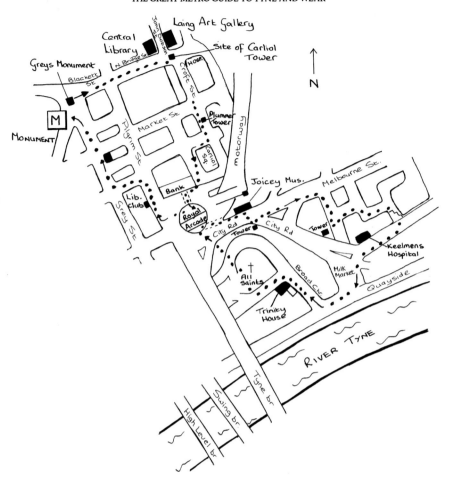

and replaced earlier premises near St John's church. It was one of several voluntary establishments which provided maternity care for the poor, in this case married women.

Close by, Dobson's New Bridge Street station, terminus of the Blyth and Tyne Railway, was demolished to make way for the motorway. Turn south alongside the Lying-in Hospital and cross Market Street to the Plummer Tower — one of the old town wall towers — now standing isolated in Croft Street (which follows the line of the wall). It was rebuilt in 1742 as a meeting room by the Ma-

sons Company. More recently it was a museum out-station. It is now closed to the public.

Now a new wall cuts the city at this point: the Central Motorway East forms a barrier between the town centre and the east, as did Pandon Dene before it was filled in the 1880s. The Pandon Burn flowed under Barras Bridge and the sites of the Civic Centre and Polytechnic through a valley of gardens and watermills before turning south to reach the Tyne near Broad Chare. New Bridge Street was constructed over the valley about 1812, via a delicately humped three-arched bridge which appears in a painting of 1821 by J Lumsden.

At the foot of Croft Street is Carliol Square, now completely filled with commercial buildings but once the site of a gaol demolished in 1925.

Turn left down the west side of the square; at the bottom corner bear right up the far side of the Bank of England. Alongside this enter subway leading to Swan House. This block, spanning the roundabout, is named after the inventor of the incandescent electric lamp. A case containing a prototype has been removed from the small central square and the commemorative fountain now runs dry.

Straight ahead enter the partial reconstruction of Dobson and Grainger's fine Royal Arcade which faced the eastern end of Mosley Street. The original was demolished in 1963, along with the ancient Friends' Meeting House next door, to make way for the roundabout. The reconstruction of part of the interior is attractive but sad — the demise of the original was widely regretted. The masonry of its exterior, which made an impressive terminal to Mosley Street, was set aside but never re-erected.

Leave the Royal Arcade by the left — notice the 19th century soup kitchen inscription in front of you. Turn right to subway leading to Joicey (Folk) Museum (closed Sunday and Monday). This attractive building, previously known as the Holy Jesus Hospital, was built in 1681 by the Corporation to care for the city's Freemen. It used to be divided up into miniature one-room flatlets where dependents could end their days. Now the rooms are furnished in the styles of various periods. The tower at the eastern end of the building is probably part of the Austin Friary, retained by the Crown after the Dissolution as a royal manor — hence the district name of Manors. The external appearance of the hospital was greatly damaged in the 1880s when City Road was constructed across its spacious piazza, and at a height well above arcade level.

Leave the museum at the far end of the arcade and cross to right hand side of road junction nearby. On the left of the white building are the remains of the Corner Tower where the wall turned east to enclose the newly-acquired area of Pandon. There's a good viewpoint by the tower from which stairs descend through planting to Cowgate. Beyond it, All Saints Church crowns a hill. Re-cross City Road and turn up Melbourne Street. The massive building on your left is the old corporation power station which provided current for trams, trolley-buses and street lighting. Turn right at the second street to reach the Wall Knoll Tower, otherwise known as the Sallyport or Carpenter's Tower. The ornate upper floor containing an attractive meeting room was added by that guild in 1716.

At the tower turn left past a car-repair workshop to reach Garth Heads and the Keelmen's Hospital. (See page 32) Garth Heads is an immense block of early mass-housing which is now let to students. Opposite is the rear of the hospital provided in 1701 by the keelmen for their dependents. Externally, at least, it is a much more attractive building. With its clock tower and "cloister" it could almost be modelled on an Oxbridge college.

Continue past the back of the Salvation Army's Palace to new housing and the revamped flats erected in the 1930s. The area is a good place to compare the different types of public housing provided over the years. Go down to City Road by way of steps at right of flats; turn right then go down slip-road past the Barley Mow.

Go down the Milk Market, past old mills and warehouses to Quayside. At the time of writing, the area to your left is marked down for large-scale development, subject to an enquiry. The few remaining old buildings will probably disappear — access along the quayside is already restricted. The finest building — the old Co-op warehouse with its arched facades and rail wagon hoists — went several years ago and the adjacent marshalling yard with its unique electric locos, one of which can be seen in the National Railway Museum in York, has been abandoned.

Turn right along the Quay, passing the new Crown Courts then right again up Broad Chare. There used to be many chares — or narrow passages — here, but most were destroyed in the great fire of 1854. Much of the city's population was packed into them, largely in slums, although there were also a number of fine houses belonging to the rich.

To your left is the Trinity Maritime Centre, a 19th century warehouse full of interesting objects and records connected with the departed shipping trade, and Trinity House, home to the city's master mariners. Pass through the archway into the Court where you will find the Chapel approached up a wide flight of steps. Founded in the 15th century, the present buildings are the result of alterations carried out at various times — the Chapel is early 17th century and its present west front, the best known part of the building, was built in 1800. The various blocks of almshouses were being added to as late as 1820. Public access to

The new Bank of England

the building has been improved recently.

Nearby in an old warehouse is the home of Live Theatre, which performs regularly, both inside, and outside in a courtyard. Barristers' chambers are being formed around some of the old courtyards — conveniently situated for the new Crown Courts.

Leave the Chare up the steep narrow street (Dog Bank) to the right of Trinity House to reach All Saints church, once the busiest church in the city but now deconsecrated. Built in 1796 to replace a medieval building, in an elegant classical style by David Stephenson, it features a spire reminiscent of Wren's or Gibbs' London work. It is one of the country's rare "circular" churches although it is, in fact, slightly elliptical in plan.

The entrance features a classical porch and a vestibule under the tower. Following slum clearance in the adjacent Silver Street, Dog Bank (now being redeveloped as housing) and other parts of the lower town, the church fell into disuse. It has been restored, however, and is now used as a music and educational resource centre. The best view is from the Quay up King Street.

The church fronts on to the foot of old Pilgrim Street. To your left, Akenside Hill was part of the Great North Road as it wound steeply up narrow streets overhung by jettied-timber houses. But turn right to find footway under the railway arch to return to the Royal Arcade. Leave the courtyard on the left (west) side subway to reach Pilgrim Street outside the old Liberal Club, once a coaching inn.

Opposite is the Bank of England, one of the city's more interesting modern buildings. Turn left down High Bridge, one of the ancient streets across the valley of the Lort Burn. Turn right up Grey Street to the Metro, passing under the great columned portico of the Theatre Royal.

South Shields

3¼ miles (including pier 5¼)
Maritime concerns predominate in this walk
around one of the world's greatest sea-faring
towns— also the home of Tyne and Wear's best
preserved Roman fort.

The Shields ferry

LEAVING South Shields Metro, turn right along King Street and its continuation, Ocean Road, noting the South Shields Museum on your right, which inside has displays of local and natural history, and the Catherine Cookson gallery.

Turn left up Baring Street (signposted "To Roman Fort") to reach the Roman remains of *Arbeia* and its museum. Re-

cent clearances have exposed more of the fort and one of the main gateways has been reconstructed to give visitors an idea of what it would have looked like. *(See page 27)*

The fort was built on a knoll with commanding views upriver and of the sea and coast. The earliest known buildings were of timber, built around 120AD. The fort was rebuilt in stone around

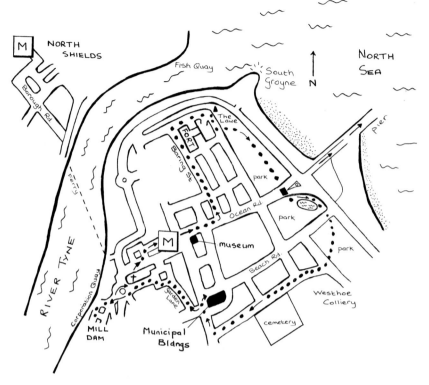

163AD and again in 208AD when it was used as a supply base for soldiers fighting in Scotland and, later, garrisons stationed along the Roman Wall. It is the only known permanent stone-built supply base of the Roman empire.

Turn right off Baring Street along the north side of the camp to the north end of the Lawe — a line of pleasant houses situated on an escarpment looking out over the harbour mouth. On the far side of the road is a pyramidal column which served as a navigational marker and, beside it, the headquarters of the Tyne Pilotage Authority and the lookout of the river pilots whose job it is to guide ships safely into the harbour.

Today, with few ships entering the river and a fast launch reducing both the time and the hazards involved, the work of this hereditary body is much restricted. In the days of the sailing colliers, however, there were many pilots, competing for work by rowing out to meet incoming ships, sometimes going as far south as Whitby. Until the construction of the twin piers last century, it could be very dangerous work.

Pass south along the Lawe and drop down into North Marine Park on your left, leading you to the end of Ocean Road. At the fork in the road is preserved the lifeboat *Tyne* one of the first to be built and a memorial to its "inventors" William Wouldhave and Henry Greathead.

The boat was the result of a competition held after the ship the *Adventure of Newcastle* grounded on the Herd Sands during a violent gale in 1789 with considerable loss of life — all within sight of helpless spectators.

A public committee was set up to commission a design for a life-saving boat offering a prize for the best submission. Both Wouldhave and Greathead sent in designs: both were rejected. After that, however, the story gets rather controversial.

The committee eventually commissioned Greathead to build a boat — which he did — and which when finished bore a striking similarity to that proposed by Wouldhave. The lifeboat won Greathead a number of awards — much to Wouldhave's disgust who claimed the design was his.

Sadly, Wouldhave died a poor man in a cottage on Nelson Bank, near Mill Dam in 1821. The bicentenary of the Lifeboat was being celebrated, at South Shields Museum until September 1990.

The left hand of the fork, Pier Parade, passes the Pavilion Theatre to the amusement park at the beginning of the pier. The pier, at almost a mile is almost twice as long as the North pier. It divides the Herd Sands into the North Foreshore, within the harbour, and the South Foreshore, without. The erection of the two piers turned a dangerous estuary into a safe harbour.

From the Pavilion, cross the road to the South Marine Park, follow the miniature railway track round the boating lake and cross Beach Road into Bents Park. Leave this on the west side and follow Sea Way and Erskine Road past the cemetery to Westoe Road — the main north to south road which changes its name several times as it runs through the town. The mass of Westoe colliery is on your left — one of the town's so called "three collieries". The other two, Hilda and Harton, have now gone.

Turn right down Westoe Road (Fowler Street) to the Municipal Buildings (1903) — the most impressive of the period in the Tyne and Wear area. *(See page 42)* South Shields became a county borough in 1888.

Opposite the Municipal Buildings go along Crossgate and turn right down Garden Lane. At the square turn left along Coronation Street to the roundabout. Beyond this is the run-down Mill Dam area where a restoration programme is underway. Several buildings at the old Corporation Quay are worth study. There is also a good view of the river from here.

Return to the roundabout beyond which is St Hilda's church — a neoclassical building of 1810 (although the tower was built in 1768), galleried on three sides with columns and arches of cast iron. The building replaced a medieval parish church which was said to be on the site of a 7th century nunnery founded by St Hilda.

Cross the road to the expansive Market Place — preferably on a Monday or Saturday when it is in use. Visit the old Town Hall in the centre — a most attractive little building with an arcaded lower storey, built at the same time as the church tower. It was badly damaged during the Blitz and fell into disrepair before being restored in 1977. It is now a listed building.

From here King Street leads straight to the Metro station, visible at high level.

The walk can be extended by two miles if a stroll along the pier is included.

Sunderland

3 miles
A short walk around both the old and
new areas of the town.

LEAVE Sunderland station to right (west exit) and turn right to pedestrian square. Turn left from square into Bridges shopping mall, passing right through it to Crowtree Road. Cross the road to the massive Leisure Centre, a rather intimidating building, and follow the pedestrian way through the Centre and the old Green or "Town Park" of Bishopwearmouth. This has now been divided up by paved walkways, though there's a secluded area at the south end.

After leaving the Leisure Centre turn right at the first intersection of paths to the parish church of St Michael and all Angels with St Hilda. The 18th century tower is the oldest part, the transepts are 19th century. Most of the church, however, was rebuilt in 1933. The nave, flanked by double aisles, is the centre of a very spacious galleried church. Church Lane, on the east of the church, which you enter from the park, is a pleasant pedestrian way with small shops.

Cross the High Street to the Empire Theatre, now publically owned and operated. Vesta Tilley, a famous Edwardian musical hall star, laid the foundation stone of this domed building. Passing right of theatre, cross car parks and A183 to a large open space sunk between pale limestone cliffs (on left of Vaux brewery). This once served the coal staithes of the Lambton Collieries, but has now been turned into a small park. Take footpath along right lip to footbridge (Gill Bridge) which crosses high above the valley, but at the near end descend steps to the lower level. Turn right to the river bank which has here been paved and landscaped. Follow this downstream to your right below high cliffs. You will see that similar treatment has been given to the north bank. Pass under the Wearmouth rail and road bridge — until the 1790s only a ferry joined the two; the famous old Wearmouth Bridge of that date, designed by Thomas Paine of *Rights of Man* fame, decorated Sunderland pottery with its characteristic pink lustre rims, now much collected. *(See page 34)*

Continue down the riverside past the old Wear Dock to Panns Bank Landing, and the timber yard. In summer, a pleasure boat runs between here and Washington Wild Fowl park. From this point you can see the slim Saxon tower of St Peter's Church on the north shore. A short distance further along the riverside road, at the site of the old ferry crossing, turn right across High Street and up James Williams Street, between the East Banker and the White Lion.

You are now in old Sunderland (that part of the land granted to St Benedict Biscop which was "sundered" by the Wear from his monastery.) Up James Williams Street is a stretch of open grassland which used to be occupied by little streets of the old shipbuilding and seafaring town. Across it can be viewed the parish church of Holy Trinity (1719) now standing isolated and exposed — cross the grass to reach it. It is quite a handsome brick building of basilica form; tall round columns divide the interior to which a palladian apse has been added. The royal arms, and those of Bishop Crewe of Durham and the Bishop of London, adorn the gallery at the other end.

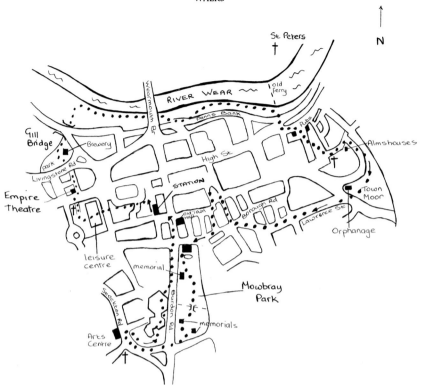

As you pass along the north side of the church (Church Walk) you will notice a small building on your right. This is the Donnison School, a parish school built in 1798 to educate 36 poor girls (rebuilt in 1827). Beyond is Trafalgar Square, containing pleasant almshouses built round three sides of a quadrangle secured by iron railings. Under the arms of Lord Nelson the "England expects" inscription continues "erected by the trustees of the Muster Roll under the IV and V of William IV, Anno Domini 1840". Appropriately, the Red Ensign is still flown from the flagstaff.

Beyond the almshouses lies the Town Moor — a rather bleak patch of grass cut up by roads and footpaths with a 1930s block of flats to the left, and the railway sidings of the Hudson Dock ahead. Turn right along the Quadrant

and where the road bends hard right take the footpath across the Moor which leads round the far side of the Orphanage, now a community centre.

From the Moor gate, cross the road and go straight up Lawrence Street past the Excelsior pub. After passing through a rebuilt area you enter a more traditional setting with little intimate streets and small churches. Borough Road comes in from your right just before you reach the Norfolk Hotel where Norfolk Street leads right to an open "square" — albeit rather elongated! Turn left through the central garden. In front of you is West Sunniside — a pleasant terrace although several of the houses have been commercialised and look rather out of place. At the south end of the garden is Manor House, now occupied by a building society. To your left, down its far side, runs Foyle Street where attractive houses are let down by their commercialised neighbours.

At the foot of Foyle Street turn right and cross Borough Road to the Library, Museum and Art Gallery (1879). Exhibits include local geology and wildlife as well as examples of manufactured products, particularly the glass and pottery for which Sunderland was famous. Behind this building is Mowbray Park. The Winter Garden used to be found between the park and lake. Unfortunately, this great glass structure was destroyed by a land-mine during the last war and never restored — the library extension now occupies the site. The park stretches beyond the lake, climbing a hill.

Climb up the hill with the War memorial to your right. Half way up a bridge crosses a deep cutting which carried the branch line to the docks. High viewpoints crown the south end of the park. Note the two statues of local heroes, General Havelock *(See page 43)* and Jack Crawford, who made his name at the Battle of Camperdown in which the Dutch fleet was destroyed during a blockade of the Dutch coast in 1797. Crawford, a keelman serving on an English admiral's flagship, climbed the mast to hold the colours aloft when the top was shot away.

Leave the park at the south west corner and go (right) down Park Road to Stockton Road, passing the Civic Centre. Across Stockton Road is the unmistakable United Reformed Church of St George, Trinity and St James with an immense hollow tower (1890). To the right of it is Grange Terrace where exhibitions are held in the Arts Centre.

Cross back over Stockton Road to the Civic Centre, opened in 1970 and accessible at right hand end of terrace. The Centre, designed by Basil Spence, Bonnington and Collins, is made up of interconnecting hexagons, subdivided right down to the triangular floor tiles. Pass through it to the north end where an involved series of ramps and steps, continuing the hexagonal theme, climb to the main entrance like an amphitheatre.

Follow Burdon Road (A1018) from the bottom of the Civic Centre steps back to the main shopping area and turn left along Athenaeum Street to the railway station. The old town hall is at the intersection of two streets, somewhat disfigured by shopfronts.

Civic Centre

Gateshead

$1^1/_4$ miles

*This town trail ends at the site of the 1990 National Garden
Festival, which should leave in its wake improved
pedestrian and cycle access to the Derwent Valley and the
hills and moors of North Durham.*

LEAVE Gateshead Metro from the upper (bus station) level. This will give you one of the best views available of the immediate locality. As you will see, little is left of the old Gateshead. To the east is the most dominant landmark — the towering multi-storey car park. This was used as a location for the Michael Caine film *Get Carter* which was filmed on Tyneside.

Head beneath it to enter the upper level of the new covered market containing a mixed range of small shops. Descend escalator to the lower level to exit on the far side. On your left is a massive concrete sculpture *Sports Day*. *(See Page 60)*

This free-standing statue by Mike Winstone is just one of many pieces of sculpture to be found in the Gateshead area, thanks to a welcome initiative by Gateshead council which is encouraging the creation of art in public places.

To your right, on the far side of the street, is Holy Trinity, one of Gateshead's two ancient churches. The main, 19th century, body of the church is now the Trinity Centre but the south aisle — the 13th century St Edmund's Chapel — has been walled off. The inner doors contain strips of glazing and, even if locked, allow a view of its interior lit by narrow lancet windows. The forecourt wall incorporates a later door surround. You can view the exterior of the chapel from the narrow street on the other side of this wall.

Ahead of you, beyond the tower blocks, you will find your way barred by roads. Turn left as far as the Magnet Social Club and cross to a rather hidden subway footpath leading between the tower blocks to pass under the lower carriageways. Continue left down the far side of these to a small landscaped area. Cross this and the road it borders to follow Oakwellgate under the railway arch. This leads you to the other old church occupying an island site high above Hillgate (where Daniel Defoe is reputed to have written *Robinson Crusoe*).

The church, St Marys, is a sorry sight. Its robust tower of 1740 no longer dominates the narrow entry to the town which wound below it from a low-level bridge. It is dwarfed instead by the great bow and abutment towers of the Tyne bridge which, in 1928, raised the road above the level of the church. Due to fire damage a few years ago, the nave and transept are blank walls unrelieved by the boarded up 14th century windows. The chancel is a shell, with tracery silhouetted against the sky and the rich woodwork which furnished it is no more. You will get no nearer than the iron railings which enclose the churchyard as the gates are padlocked to secure numerous piebald horses which roam among the tombs. At the north east corner there is a mausoleum to the Green family which rises out of the trampled ground. It was designed by Robert Trollop of York.

Cross Church Street to the foot of Bottle Bank and cross also this narrow street to reach the landscaped slope which falls steeply to Pipewellgate, here separated from the river by a depot. Follow the

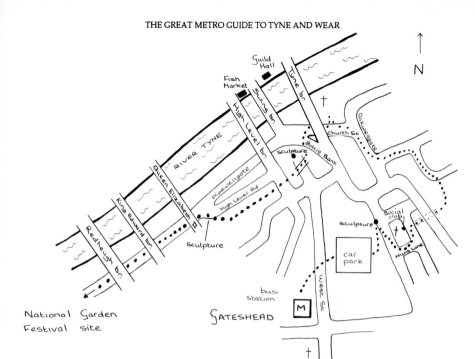

footpath as it passes under the perforated steel arches and stone abutments which form one of the large scale "sculptures" commissioned for the Borough. *(See page 60)* Continue westwards along this footpath which climbs and falls as it borders the base of the old railway works where so many great locomotives were born.

Before passing through a small arch in the abutment of Robert Stephenson's High Level bridge, pause to examine this cast iron structure and to look back on the Tyne bridge, below which is moored a vast floating nightclub. You are looking down upon Armstrong's hydraulic Swing bridge built on the traditional river crossing point from Roman times. At the far end, the building to the left with a large coat of arms, is the old fish market; that on its right is the historic Newcastle Guildhall. Beyond these are the surviving timber-framed mansions of the gentry and richer merchants, above which the por-

ticoed Moot Hall stands on the lip of the Castle mound.

Once more in the open beyond the archway you will see the Queen Elizabeth II bridge which carries the Metro between the tunnels which convey it under Newcastle and Gateshead. The original Gateshead-Carlisle railway terminated near where you stand.

Where the tree-planted slopes of the Rabbit Banks narrow, turn down under the *Rolling Moon* by Colin Rose — another sculpture commissioned by Gateshead council. It consists of a globe mounted off-centre on a high arch. Turn left along the riverside road leading to the Garden Festival site. Overhead, the King Edward bridge carries the main London to Newcastle line and the new Redheugh bridge bears a four-lane road connecting the western side of the town centres. Unlike the other bridges over the Tyne, this is of reinforced concrete.

Just after the new bridge is the south abutment of the old bridge, now a viewing platform.

Two new sculptures should appear along the river bank during 1990.

Here you reach the Garden Festival site. After the Festival has closed there will be a footway up the Team Valley as far as the entrance to the trading estate at Lobley Hill. Another route will be created on or near to the bank of the Tyne to Derwent Haugh and up the Derwent Valley to the Derwent Walk along the old Consett railway.

Retrace your steps to return to Gateshead Metro.

The south bank: the Rolling Moon sculpture is to the left and the Queen Elizabeth II "Metro" bridge on the right.

COASTAL WALKS

The above walks can be linked to provide a trail from one end of the Tyne and Wear coast to the other

Shiremoor to Seaton Sluice

12 miles (approx.)

Before mining make its mark, the Shire Moor used to be a desolate place, dreaded by travellers although crossed by the old Salters Way. You can still walk the old miners' tracks often without meeting a soul even though the land is now farmed. The middle reaches of the Seaton Burn are equally unvisited.

FROM Shiremoor Metro turn left, past short terrace, and take footpath to left. Pass round school on right to Earsdon Road. Turn left along shopping street and then right between bathroom shop and Masonic Hall on right up Moor Edge Road. After Moor Edge Farm bear right along lane, past road to Backworth, to signposted farm road.

Just before track turns right, take footpath to left reaching side of railway.(This is the old Blyth and Tyne railway, now little used except as a diversion). Follow this before turning right through alder plantation by fenced path across reclaimed land. The fenced footpath ends at corner of large field containing two electricity pylons. Head between these for solitary bush, keeping to left of this to avoid ponds to right. Bear right and head for field corner, aiming just right of grey and red factory in far distance. This field is arable and the footpath may pass through crops. Keep to it as closely as possible.

Upon reaching wooded valley, bear right along path through beech woods. Cross pack-horse bridge and turn right along open space between stream and estate keeping as near the stream as practicable. After about $^1/_2$ mile you reach an old wagonway embankment — use this to recross stream. At end of embankment turn left on to second track and double back to regain valley. Follow it down, crossing bridge, to steps leading up to Dale Top and Holywell Village.

Leave main road where it turns down right to bridge — note old house at corner. Go along Holywell Dean Road to end of houses and turn left, look for footpath exit (top left corner from you). Follow footpath, turning right to pass ponds on your left (popular with migrating and nesting birds). Cross embankment of old Avenue Branch railway to junction of farm tracks. Take that which carries straight ahead. This is based on a very old plateway which brought coal to Seaton Sluice and Hartley for export or use in salt and glass making. The track on the left leads to Seaton Delaval Hall.

To your left is an obelisk — one of two erected on the Seaton Delaval estate. There are various legends about their origins but they were probably "follies". The one remaining has been built on the axis of the Hall which you can see in the distance. The hall was built for the Delaval family in 1707 to Sir John Vanburgh's design. On its left is a Norman church, on its right the orangery and mausoleum — unfortunately vandalised. (For a closer view take the track leading left and return to this intersection. *This will add an extra mile in each direction.*)

The track turns right to Hartley West Farm but continue on wagonway towards Seaton Sluice. The wagonway

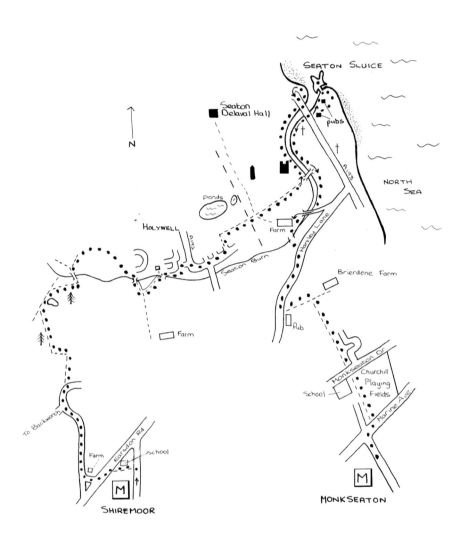

used to enter Seaton Sluice by a high bridge but this has long since gone. At the end of the abutment, descend by steps to stream and turn left. In a few yards you reach, on your left, the ruins of Starlight Castle which, once again, has been reduced by vandalism. This "folly" was reputed to have been erected overnight to surprise the guests at Seaton Delaval Hall: they got many other surprises, not all pleasant, including hidden fountains among the garden paths to drench the unwary.

The path leads past woods down the valley, here tidal. Pass under the road bridge then follow the quayside. Turn left at the mouth of the stream and return to main road along track. The hill on your right is one of flint ballast brought back by returning colliers to what was then the main coal-exporting harbour. Erosion has now almost removed the ballast.

Cross by the road bridge and walk above the harbour. There is a good view point opposite the Waterford Arms although the headland was more picturesque before the cottages there were demolished. As you walk along to the King's Arms there is an unfolding view up the long beach to Blyth. The great rock cutting on your left was formed in the middle of the 18th century to improve the harbour. At its seaward end it is just possible to identify the foundations of the crane used to lift a portcullis, This was used to maintain the water level after high tides, so it could be released later to "sluice" out the harbour — hence Seaton Sluice.

Cross the footbridge and circle the headland before returning to the main road. Cross road and take footpath on left of church. Follow this along the burn edge. At stone bridge a farm road will lead you further up the valley. Before Hartley West Farm take left branch to pass below the farm by the ruins of a mill. About 300 yards beyond the mill, cross footbridge and climb to Hartley Lane (B1325). Follow this right to Bee Hive Inn.

At left corner of car park, stile leads into an unimproved meadow rich in plants. Follow path along left edge and continue to Briar Dene Farm where the bed of the Avenue Branch railway can be followed (to right) to Monkseaton. Leave it through the playing fields on left. The station is on your right.

The North Tyneside coast

10 miles

A bracing walk along rugged coastline to the busy North Shields harbour visiting an island lighthouse and a fortified priory. The walk can be shortened by catching the Metro at a number of intermediate stations. Alternatively you can pick up the walk at Tynemouth station for a short trail around the town.

FROM Monkseaton station bridge turn down Marine Avenue and left into Churchill Playing Fields. Cross these northwards to leave at north west corner by track of old Avenue Branch railway. Pass under Monkseaton Drive and follow track for a further $^3/_4$ mile. Ahead of you is Brier Dene Farm. A footpath will take you to right of farm, crossing a small bridge and, in a short distance, to path running east north east from the farm, now on your left.

Turn right along path for $^1/_4$ mile then turn left along line of former Collywell Bay electric railway branch to stone abutments of dismantled railway bridge (golf course on right). Turn right between them to reach main coastal road at corner, continue down it, keeping cemetery wall on right. At next corner cross into minor road leading to St Mary's Island which should be followed to first car park. Turn left along nature trail track at field edge. In season, the field is a gathering ground for flocks of birds, mainly lapwing, curlew, oystercatchers

St Mary's Island

96

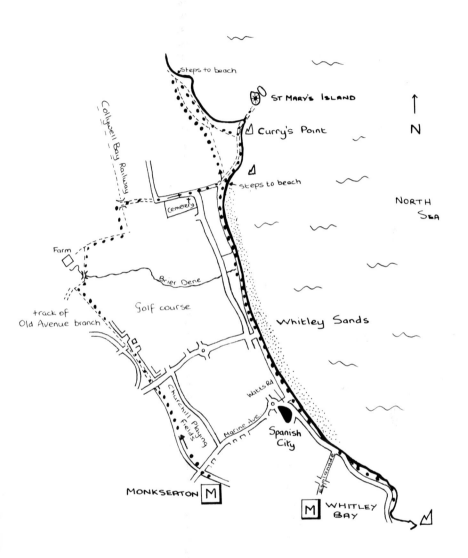

Steps to beach

St Mary's Island

Curry's Point

steps to beach

Collywell Bay Railway

Cemetery

NORTH SEA

Farm

Brier Dene

Golf course

Whitley Sands

track of Old Avenue branch

Watts Rd

Churchill Playing Fields

Marine Ave

Spanish City

MONKSEATON Ⓜ

Ⓜ WHITLEY BAY

Esplanade

N

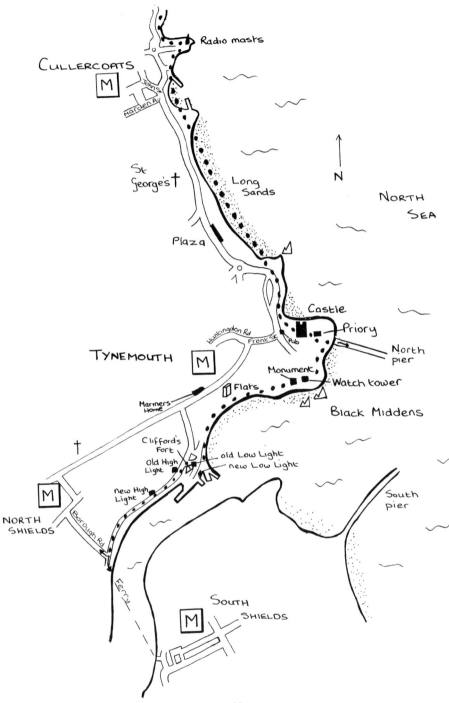

and other waders. Past the old rifle butts are steps down to the base of the cliffs which are here very insecure but of great interest to geologists. Turn back southwards but keep to left, following coastal path.

Reaching the causeway end, at Curry's Point note the plaque commemorating the execution in 1739 of Michael Curry for the murder of a local innkeeper. The body hung there long enough to give his name to the promontory. Nearby there is a tide table, necessary when crossing the causeway to St Mary's Island as it cannot be reached at high tide. Most of the island is now taken up by the lighthouse—the Whitley Bay emblem — and staff quarters. The now-redundant lighthouse has been acquired for public use and can be climbed if desired — although such a feat is not for the faint-hearted— or encircled by the footpath below the cliffs. There are also information displays in the staff quarters.

After returning across the causeway follow the promenade down the coast to your left. Try spotting the numerous, yet well-camouflaged, birds which feed among the rocks and seaweed below. If the tide is out the beach can be reached by steps at the end of the promenade; otherwise you must take the path along the cliff top. **Note:** These cliffs are dangerous, keep away from the edge!

Past Brier Dene there is a second length of promenade — this passes the Panama Swimming Club where hardy members can often be seen braving the mid-winter chill of the North Sea. Just past it, at the Panama Dip, a ramp leads up to the Spanish City funfair with its white dome a well-known local landmark — given wider fame by the rock band Dire Straits in their song, *Tunnel of Love* — and visible as you make your way from the island. From here the coast can be followed by a mixture of promenade and coastal road, passing above

the Table Rocks tidal swimming pool, to the headland bearing the Cullercoats marine radio masts.

The promenades at each side of the headland are connected by steps to a passageway between the radio station and the houses. Little is left of the quaint old fishermen's village which, during the last century, was a gathering place for artists collectively known as the "Cullercoats School".

From the look-out there is a good view down to the little sandy harbour. It is now used only for fishing boats but at one time coal, salt and other products were exported from here. A ramp leads down to the beach which can, tide permitting, be crossed to the next headland. The brick building at the back of the bay is the Dove Marine Laboratory, part of Newcastle University. The cliff beyond contains caves and these are sometimes accessible, tide and sand level permitting.

The sea edge can be followed to St George's Church, built by the Duke of Northumberland in 1884. Its magnificent spire is another famous coastal landmark. From here follow, if possible, the Long Sands — a fine beach backed by the remains of sand dunes. Above the beach is the gaunt grey Plaza, built in 1878 to provide more sophisticated entertainment for the early tourists enticed to the coast by the salt water bathing and mineral springs. Behind it is the park with boating lake. The Long Sands end at Sharpness Point above the open air swimming bath; beyond is the sheltered King Edward's Bay nestling between it and the castle promontory.

Reaching the neck of the rocky peninsular, at the Gibraltar Rock pub, a curving road across the dry moat leads to the great gateway to the Priory ruins behind the castle's defensive screen. Only the landward side of the Priory promontory was fortified. The gatehouse and parts of the flanking walls remain, albeit with obvious rebuilding in parts. (See page 28)

The ruins are approached through this defensive barbican which ends the vista down the wide Front Street of the old village. For visitors arriving by sea, the tall east end of the Priory is their first landmark. The sight must have been even more breathtaking when the great Priory was intact and before the days of high buildings which now form a backdrop. Even in its present state, it dominates many stormy seascape paintings.

In the seventh century, St Oswald rebuilt King Edwins Chapel. In 651 King Oswyn was the first King to be buried in the precinct — King Malcolm of Scotland, successor to Macbeth, was also buried there at the end of the 11th century.

Destroyed by the Danes in the ninth century, the Priory was refounded in 1090 and the original structure built during the following 20 years. Most of today's ruins date from later alterations.

In the 14th century the Priory entertained several royal visitors, both English and Scottish. In 1539 the Priory buildings were given up to the Crown and demolished, leaving only that part used as the Parish Church. This started to collapse in 1659 and was abandoned nine years later.

Visit the only portion remaining intact — the tiny vaulted chapel at the east end of the church (obtain the key from the English Heritage shop in the barbican). The headland has now been cleared of most of the later buildings, but a new coastguard building has just been opened and nearby gun emplacements can be visited.

From the castle, descend hill on right of moat to small bay containing yacht and rowing clubs. Follow footpath at foot of castle cliffs to pier gates, the base of the naval gun emplacement on your left provides an excellent viewpoint along the outer face of the north pier,

particularly if there's a swell running from the north east. At low tide you can see the remains of the earlier, shorter pier which was breached by a storm.

This is the start for a bracing walk along the pier if you so wish, but this will add $1/_2$ mile each way to the walk (closed in heavy seas).

Returning down the slope from the pier gates, turn left through fence into Prior's Haven and ascend access road to the dip between the two headlands. Follow road to left on to the Spanish Battery. The naval guns have now been removed but their bases can be seen around the top of the mound which encircles the Battery. This is an excellent point from which to view the coast southwards, with views also up the valley as far as Gateshead. The remains of a jetty to be seen at the near end of the North pier mark the terminus of the ferry service which used to run right down the river from Newcastle prior to the electrification of the railway in the early years of this century.

Leave the Battery on the south side to reach the end of the promenade which leads to the Fish Quay. On your left, the railings bear a plaque recording some of the shipping disasters which occurred here before the erection of piers to shelter the mouth of the estuary. The Black Midden rocks have been reduced but enough remain to harbour many sea birds at some stages of the tide; two ships have had to be removed off the rocks in recent years.

On your right is the Collingwood monument. A massive plinth supports this statue — built by local sculptor, Lough in the 1840s — of Admiral Lord Collingwood who was born in Newcastle and succeeded Lord Nelson at Trafalgar.

The wooden building to your right is the watch tower from which the safety of ships was monitored by the Volunteer Life Brigade founded in 1864; there is a small museum (not open Mondays). *(See page 36)* The harbour mouth is over-looked by the massive Ralph Knott flats dating from the 1930s. *(See page 49)* Opposite is the Groyne with its little lighthouse and warning bell, separat-ing the river from the North Foreshore.

The estuary walk ends at the remains of the jetty which led to the Lloyd's hailing station made redundant by more modern methods of communication. Prior to radio , all shipping movements were monitored by Lloyds and ships travelling in and out past the little cabin were interrogated.

On your right is a cluster of buildings associated with the fishing industry and now being restored with aid from the European Community. The buildings include the old Low Light tower, which, with the old High Light on the high ground, acted as guides for ships enter-ing the river mouth.

Around the old Low Light are the remains of Clifford's Fort (1672) which superceded Tynemouth Castle as the centre of local defence. Much of the stone perimeter wall remains along with some of the upper brick breastwork con-taining gun ports. Pass round the river end of the fort by the lifeboat house. On your right is the "new" Low Light built when the navigable channel changed course.

The fishing boats in the fish dock and along the Union Quay are of many shapes and sizes. Their registration let-ters refer to various ports in Britain and the near Continent, including many from Scotland. From the Quay there is a good view of the new High Light, an elegant balconied tower used as a dwelling house until recently — note the cliff fish "sculpture" alongside it. The steep banks running down to the quay used to har-bour a mass of stairs, alleyways and slum property while the higher level ground was filled with fine terraces and squares — little trace remains of either.

A nondescript road leads along to the next view of the river. One of the build-ings on your left can be identified as the old *Wooden Doll*, a pub taking its name from a ship's figure-head. It is now re-established on higher ground above the fish dock. Reaching Borough Road there is a welcome change in the environ-ment. The New Quay and Market Place, which the Duke of Northumberland built to provide an imposing water-borne en-trance to the town, have been tidied up and eating places and antique shops abound as you make your way to the Shields ferry* — should you wish to continue this walk along the South Tyneside coast *(see next walk)*. Otherwise take a bus from the ferry landing, or climb Borough Road turning right on main road, to reach North Shields Metro station.

The ferries run every 30 minutes; the crossing takes about seven minutes.

South Shields to Sunderland

5 miles

This varied walk from Tyne to Wear links the industrial scenery of the rivers' ports via the marvellous sands and cliffs of the South Tyneside coast.

IF continuing the coastal walk from North Shields, after alighting from the Shields Ferry go up to Ferry Street then turn left, passing the Alum House on your left. A plaque records the early history of this building and its association with the lead industry. Continue northwards along River Drive, a high-level road skirting the mound on which the Romans built their fort, and where there are good views across the river to North Shields.

If you are starting the walk from South Shields Metro, follow instructions in South Shields town trail until you reach the fort.

Pass Graving Docks on left and follow the road around the curving south bank. On the right of where the road loops round the docks is the old South Shields station and at the dip spanned by the bow bridge, the old South Shields electric railway terminated. Keep to right by the houses, (Greens Place) remaining on high ground and overlooking the Wapping shore.

At the corner where the road turns southwards, note the pyramidal navigational marker and descend to the lower level. Walk out to the little red lighthouse on the South Groyne then follow the North Foreshore to the South pier — about a mile in length should you want to walk it.

From the Watch House at the beginning of the pier, follow the promenade behind amusement park and continue to the Gypsies Green Sports Stadium, or follow the shoreline if tides permit.

The name of the railway carriage restaurant *Rattler* between the south promenade and Sea Road commemorates the old coast railway — known as the *Marsden Rattler*. From this point, there are a number of paths which can be followed along the cliffs, and across the "leas". This stretch of coast has been given to the National Trust by the local authority. Note the evocative names of local features such as Frenchman's Bay, Velvet Beds and Man Haven. Frenchman's Bay is so called because a ship from France was wrecked there years ago. The history of the coastline is steeped in smuggling stories and legends such as those of the "Hairy Man", a young sailor said to have lived like a caveman at Marsden Bay, and "Willie the Rover". Willie also lived in a cave, but at Frenchman's Bay, and survived by eating shellfish. He was eventually driven away by local fishermen after stealing from their mussel beds.

Also, look out for plaques along the route which give information about the flora, fauna, geology and wildlife to be found in the area.

The 100 foot high Marsden Rock is the largest and best known of the rock stacks along this stretch of coast. The area is also a designated nature reserve. Tunnels, worn through it, can be explored at low tide. There used to be a stairway to the top which is a great

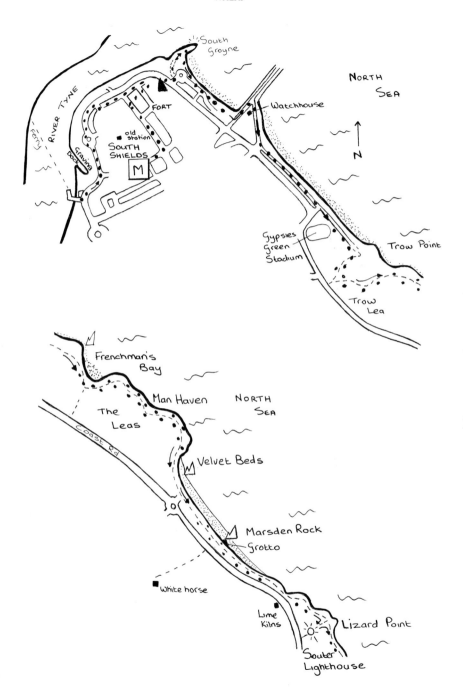

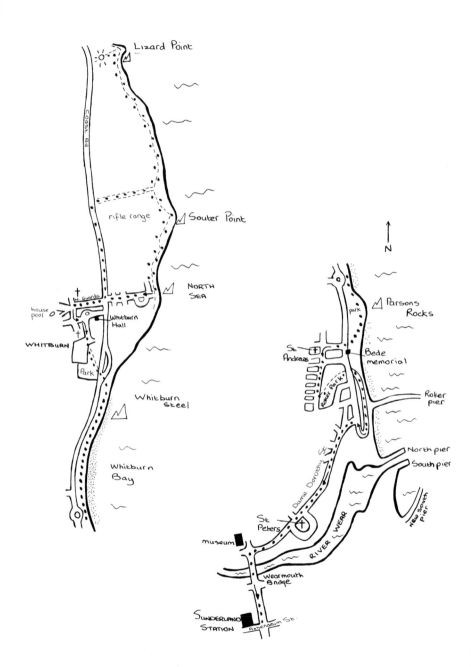

haunt of cormorants — more than 10 per cent of the English breeding population are said to nest on top of the Rock. The cliffs of the bay are, in season, white with fulmars and kittiwakes — more than 4,000 pairs of kittiwakes breed in this area.

Access to the beach is by stairs by the entrance to the Grotto pub There is also a lift available in the pub for a small charge.

The Grotto itself has features of interest, including a bar built into the cliff face. The place was originally built in 1782 by a local quarry worker — Jack the Blaster, for his family to live in. It was converted, around 30 years later, into a 15-roomed house by Peter Allan, a gamekeeper to the Marquis of Londonderry. After his death in 1849 it developed into the public house and restaurant which it is today.

The ghost of John the Jibber, a smuggler, is said to haunt the Grotto and the publican is reputed to leave a glass of beer out for him every night.

The limestone caves have been used for less innocent purposes including smuggling and imprisonment.

A picture of a white horse has been scratched out of a quarry face with tar and limewash in the Cleadon Hills half a mile inland at Marsden Quarry and can be seen from the lane running inland from the Grotto.

The cliffs continue a further two miles beyond Souter Point, the most eastern headland on this coast. Half way along however, is Lizard Point, distinguished by its lighthouse confusingly called Souter Light to differentiate it from the Cornish Lizard. The National Trust has acquired buildings at the lighthouse and will probably be opening an information centre and other facilities there in the future.

Note the massive lime kilns, preserved on the far side of the road, which used to be fed from the quarries behind.

The next stretch of clifftop used to be disfigured by colliery workings. These have now been cleared and are being landscaped. However, opposite Souter Point, there is a Ministry of Defence firing range. Obviously, if firing is in progress, make a detour along the road, and continue to Whitburn. This old village is one of the most pleasant in the area and well worth a visit. A path leads westwards, from the sea edge along Ash Grove and Rackley Way onto East Mill Lane — the coast road.

Cross the road and continue along North Guards, turning left at the House Pool to reach Front Street. Turn left and then right into Church Lane. Note the well-positioned houses along the route.

Further along Front Street, just beyond Church Lane, is Whitburn Hall —

Souter lighthouse

an interesting building of many periods. Its owners, the Williamsons, did much to preserve the village. The family held the Hedworth title and the seventh and eighth baronets were local MPs. The white horse, *(see above)* at Marsden Quarry is said to commemmorate the death of Lady Williamson who disappeared while out riding by the sea.

Continue down Church Lane and note the buildings including a 13th century church and bow-fronted rectory. At the end of the lane, take the footpath across the little park which contains a statue of Lewis Carroll who often visited the village and composed his nonsense rhyme, *The Walrus and the Carpenter* while staying here. The path brings you back to the coast road which it meets opposite a tiny concealed haven containing fishing boats. The 17th century hamlet now consists of modern houses.

The rocks of Whitburn Steel point far out to sea and can be explored at low tide but, beware as the sea encircles the rocks before covering them.

L S Lowry spent his last years here, painting seascapes. Half a mile of sands, backed by a promenade, lead to Parson's Rocks where a small park separates the front from the road. Quarter of a mile further on is the Bede Memorial, but first go up Rock Lodge Road on the right to visit the Church of St Andrew, a most astounding church dating from the early years of this century and described by Sir John Betjeman as "a bold and imaginative experiment which has triumphantly succceeded".

It has also been called a cathedral to the Arts and Crafts movement. Built out of rough stone, it features inside a huge cruciform space spanned by great arches.

Glass and furnishings by leaders of the Arts and Crafts movement include Burne-Jones tapestries, carpets from the William Morris workshop, a font by Randall Wells and chancel murals by Macdonald Gill.

Go south a short distance down Roker Park Road and enter the park on your left. Follow the valley down towards the sea returning to the sea front by subway. Turn left, if you wish, to resume sea walk at the Bede memorial. A quarter of a mile walk along the promenade will bring you to Roker pier.

Unlike the Tyne, the mouth of the Wear has an outer basin almost enclosed by the curving arms of the Roker and New South piers. The actual mouth lies within these, confined in a narrow space between the shorter, and older, piers, marked by a small lighthouse.

Although the river has been devoted mainly to shipbuilding and the export of coal, cargo handling has taken place in the Hudson and Hendon Docks which were provided with a second outlet be-

St Peters Church

106

tween the South West pier and the confusingly-named North East pier. This mile-long range of docks and their associated railways, cuts the town centre off from the sea.

Just past Roker pier the road swings to the right along Harbour View and Dame Dorothy Street, separated from the river by docks and abandoned shipyards. Follow this for $^3/_4$ mile, to arrive at St Peter's Church on your left. *(See page 28)*

In the new Chapter House you can learn about the 1,300 year-old history of Benedict Biscop's monastery: how the local nobleman made five journeys to Rome, bringing back books and ideas; and how he brought French craftsmen to help in the building of the twin monasteries of Monkwearmouth and Jarrow — a great community of 600 monks of whom Bede was the most famous.

The ancient church was founded in 675 although the present building includes the west wall of the original church together with a typical narrow Saxon tower built around 900 upon an earlier vaulted west porch. The chancel and north doorway date from the 14th century, the north aisle from the 19th century. The church can be viewed daily except when services are in progress.

Continue along the north bank for nearly half a mile to Wearmouth Bridge. Almost opposite you just before the bridge is Monkwearmouth Station Museum which contains a collection of rail vehicles and other transport memorabilia (closed Monday). It is housed in Dobson's elegant little station of 1848.

Cross the bridge and continue straight on for Sunderland station. The present bridge, built in 1929, replaced a much more elegant structure and one with an interesting history. Though modified by Stephenson in 1858, the original bridge was designed by Thomas Paine, better known as a political philosopher. *(See page 44)* Only a ferry joined Monkwearmouth and Bishop Wearmouth until the 1790s when Paine's bridge was erected, largely due to the patronage of Rowland Burdon of Castle Eden Hall, Member of Parliament for the county.

Paine had designed the bridge for a river in Philadelphia but failed to get it built before he left America. His opportunity came during his stay in Britain and before he left to live in France. Unfortunately, the bridge was denied the immortality achieved by his famous book, *The Rights of Man*, and made way for something more suited to modern-day traffic. Next to the iron bridge over the Severn, Paine's was the oldest iron bridge in existence and incidentally, designed with a greater appreciation of the qualities of the material.

Note: Every autumn, Sunderland illuminations stretch from the Wearmouth Bridge to the boundary just south of Whitburn and including Roker Park.

Sunderland to Ryhope

9 miles

*This scenic walk visits one of the country's most
distinctive examples of Victorian industrial architecture
— the Ryhope Pumping station.*

FROM the south exit of Sunderland station turn right along Brougham Street then left down Crowtree Road to Vine Place which leads to a roundabout on the New Durham Road (A690). Keep to right of this road and turn up Western Hill. On left, a footpath over the Knoll will give access to the old wagonway which led to the Lambton Staithes. To the left, a paved path follows this track just west of the Durham Road to the gyratory traffic system round the site of the Barnes Hotel. As the tunnel under the road has been closed, the path is broken by traffic flow, re-entry is from the left hand end of the hotel forecourt.

Continue along track through the Plains Farm district, keeping straight on at the nurseries to follow the left edge of housing (Perth Road) into the Sports and Recreation Centre created out of the old Silksworth Colliery. Pass between the two lakes then climb the hill to the ski slope. To the left of this and beside Silksworth Lane is the entry to another wagonway which led to the main docks. Take this track along the northern fringe of Tunstall to cross Tunstall Hope Road to the south of the Tunstall Hills which (to your left) rise, as the Maiden Paps, to 500 feet.

Where the open space begins to narrow, watch for exit on right up Brick Row. Cross the main road (B1286) to end of Cheviot Lane and take footpath on left of cricket field fence. This will lead down the back of Beavan Avenue to Burdon Lane. Here, turn left down the hill some 300 yards to a narrow entry on the right, at the near side of the cemetery. At the end of this, veer right across field to far corner to enter Waterworks Road. Turn right up to reservoir entrance.

The high pumping station and its even higher chimney are distinctive features of this Victorian building, sited on a level grassy plateau under which are further reservoirs. In 1869 two 100hp beam engines, manufactured by Hawthorn's of Newcastle, were commissioned to pump water up sinkings in the limestone. They were operated until 1967. After the works were abandoned, a charitable trust was set up to renovate and preserve the station. Volunteers operate one of the engines at limited times, usually bank holiday weekends from Easter to August and the late October school holiday weekend. The buildings are open from Easter to Christmas on Saturdays and Sundays, but the pumps may not be in steam. In addition to the huge architectural engines there is a museum devoted to water supply and sanitation.

Leave the site by Waterworks Road and continue down Stockton Road, bearing right at the main road junction to enter Ryhope village. Turn right on the main (Seaham) road but before going under the railway bridge, at the right hand end of the red brick blocks on your left and opposite Railway pub, take narrow lane, Ryhope Beach Road, through a confined tunnel. This leads down a small dene to the sea. From the foot of this there are good cliff views to Seaham Pier on the right and Salterfen Rocks to the left.

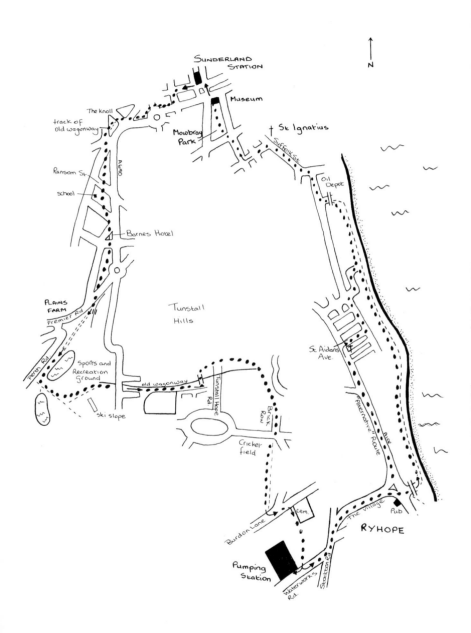

At the time of writing a problem existed at this point in the walk. The cliff top footpath was closed on safety grounds. An alternative was the main road up the coast from Ryhope Village (A1018), for a distance of a mile, to St Aidan's Avenue, opposite the cemetery, where there is a crossing over the main railway. Then turn left over grass to Ocean Road and follow this down towards the sea. It is possible to walk at low tide along the stony beach below the crumbling cliff, but this should only be attempted on a falling tide as there is no escape up the cliffs and little chance of alerting help. Perhaps the footpath may be restored when you visit.

Follow Ocean Road down to the promenade at the shoreline, or to the footpath above it. These extend some 600 yards northwards before the way is blocked by an oil depot. At some time in the future, possibly 1992, it is hoped that the seaside walk can be extended past this obstacle to the Hendon Docks, as the abandoned railway line from the docks to the town centre is to be converted into a walkway — this is the track visible in a deep cutting across Mowbray Park before it passes under the Civic Centre car park to Park Lane.

Meanwhile, you must leave the coast at the oil depot, passing up a narrow access way under the railway to Commercial Road. Turn right along this road and then left beyond the school along Robinson Terrace. At its end turn right along Suffolk Street to St Ignatius' Church, a tall structure of 1889 with an impressive interior.

Turn left up Mowbray Road and then right along Park Place, pleasant terraces with a wide central avenue which covers the main railway line. Enter Mowbray Park — the main railway actually runs underneath this — cross railway cutting and continue down to the lake. Exit at left of lake and museum and continue up Fawcett Street to Brougham Street and the station.

Ryhope Pumping station

WALKS
NORTH OF THE TYNE

Kenton to Wylam

15 miles (Return)
(Distance halved if return made by British Rail from Wylam)
A long but stimulating walk — particularly for those with an interest in the area's railway heritage. Some of the route follows old wagonways which used to carry coals to the Tyne.

LEAVE Bank Foot station by access road and turn left up Station Road. After about 300 yards, and beyond the overpass, turn right along farm road. Leave it for estate road on left before farmhouse.

After half a mile the road swings left; just after the bend take footpath on right to Whorlton Hall, crossing golf course to farm lane opposite. Pass hall by the left to reach road, going straight on for a few yards before road turns sharply right. At the bend take footpath on left along line of old wagonway. The signpost reads "Stamfordham Road and North Walbottle", but at Stamfordham Road the continuation has been fenced off. Judging by the damage to the fence, and the clear path through the plantation beyond, many people still use this route, coming out at North Walbottle by an iron kissing gate.

The alternative is to turn left until access is gained to the estate on your right, passing through it near its right-hand boundary, to leave alongside the iron gate. Take the wagonway footpath opposite, signposted "Blucher", past site of Coronation Pit, to tunnel under the A69 and reach the old Carlisle Road. Cross road and continue along wagonway on the far side of pedestrian crossing, past site of Blucher Pit to Hospital Lane. Turn right down to main road and then left to the A6085.

When the old North Wylam line has been turned into a long-distance footpath it will be worth following the wagonway past the hospital to join it at Lemington, giving a closer view of the 18th century glass cone. *(See page 33)*

Turn right into Newburn and visit the church, pleasantly sited above the street. Note the crescent shapes carved on the cottages, which denote that they are, or were, the property of the Duke of Northumberland. The church dates back to before the Conquest, but much of the building is from the 12th century, with a good deal of renovation from the last century. George Stephenson was married here, and William Hedley buried. *(See below)*

Newburn may be small, but it boasts a rich history. It is the lowest fording point on the Tyne and traces of a paved causeway, presumably Roman, have been found. In 1072 the deposed Earl of Northumberland besieged and ultimately killed the usurper in the church, burning it in the process.

In the 14th century, David II, King of Scotland, forded the river here before he was captured at Neville's Cross. Nearly 300 years later, in 1640, the ford was once again used by the Scots, this time after a battle in which *they* defeated the forces of the Bishop of Durham. The Scots, under General Lesley, were reckoned to outnumber the bishop's troops by four to one. Today, battle-site walks are held periodically.

From the church go south across the main road into Station Road. Cross the

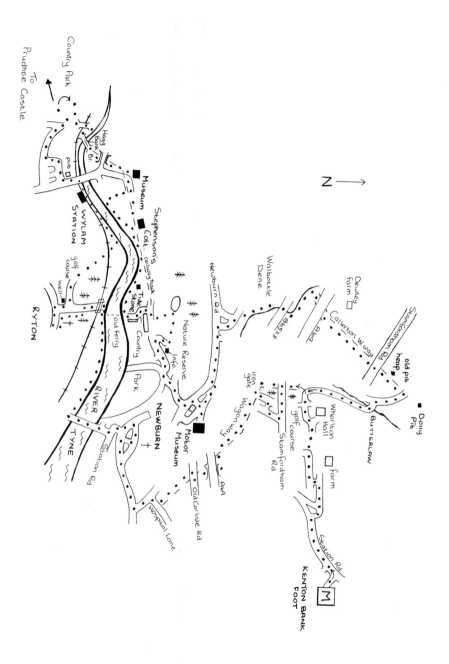

bridge over the Tyne and take the footpath to right along the river bank.

Keep a look out for the distinctive 13th century lead-covered spire of Ryton church in the distance.

After a mile, at the old ferryman's white cottage, leave the river and cross the railway (1835) by stiles near level crossing.

Climb up to the village by a lane, branching left up a wooded valley; notice the fine beech wood on left. Until the last war many people in the towns further down the river travelled by boat up to Ryton Willows to visit the fair, held on the riverside haugh you have crossed.

Ryton church is to the left. Although the church is best known for its spire, it also contains interesting carvings and brasses. Adjacent is the huge Elizabethan rectory, the east side disguised by a new facade added during the Georgian period.

There are several other impressive houses in the old part of the village. Note the well by the restored pound for stray animals at the head of the lane by which you reached the village.

Take the little road to right of well, signposted "Golf Club". A quarter of a mile past Club entrance, it becomes a lane which turns right towards the river to end at sheds. Follow path signposted "Maryside Hill" then bear left to plantations, keeping them on your right. Cross railway and head north for river (second club-house to your left). Follow riverside path to left, reaching South Wylam station. *Those not wanting to make the return journey by foot should take the train from here to Newcastle Central and then the Metro back to Kenton.*

Cross road and railway at level crossing and take estate road on south side of pub. Take second left to Wylam Wood Road and follow this road right to the Country Park.

See footnote

Return to cottages and cross the Hagg

Bank bow-string railway bridge which looks like a miniature Tyne bridge. Follow the track eastwards to the site of North Wylam station, now a car park and picnic area.

In Falcon Terrace, just to the north, is the Wylam Railway Museum, which is devoted to local railway history — and what a history! It was here that George Stephenson — often referred to as the father of the railways — was born. Here too *Puffing Billy*, the oldest surviving locomotive in the world — now in the Science Museum, London — was built in 1813 by William Hedley and Timothy Hackworth. *(See page 11)*

The North Wylam line was laid in 1876 on a wagonway of 1748; it was closed in 1968. From the car park continue eastwards either along the railway track or along the riverbank to the cottage where George Stephenson was born in 1781. He would grow up surrounded by the machines and workings of the coal mining industry, educating himself and acquiring the skills which would make him one of the world's greatest engineering pioneers.

The 18th century building is now in the care of the National Trust, and one room is open to the public most summer afternoons.

Continue along the riverside — look out for the Tide Stone which marks the tidal limit of the Tyne, 19 miles from the river mouth — until you reach Ryton ferry. Turn left here, past terraced houses, cross railway track and go behind next terrace to reach footpath leading up to nature reserve ponds. At far side of these turn right for about 300 yards to minor road. Follow it to right past an old industrial site to cottages, then turn left along rail track to Riverside Park Information Centre.

Leave by main access road, the site of Water Row Pit where Stephenson worked in 1798. Turn left off Grange Road up Westmacott Street — very steep

— to the main road. Take narrow road on left of police station opposite and slightly to your left. Turn left again along Alnwick Street, then right along Townfield Gardens to the Motor Museum, which is open most days until early evening.

Return by way of Townfield Gardens to main road and up it to Mayfield Avenue on the right. Go along this to second entry into Walbottle/Throckley Dene. Follow Dene path to old Carlisle road, cross it and continue. At head of Dene pass under trunk road by subway, bearing right about a quarter of a mile then turn left to the Callerton wagonways. The wagonways go over Walbottle Moor, part of the Duke of Northumberland's mining system of the 1770s.

The left fork is to Dewley Pit, home of George Stephenson during the 1790s, and continues over Greenwich moor. But you take the right fork over two fields, partly on an embankment. At another fork, again take the right branch along the embankment to reach the stile at Stamfordham Road. Cross stile opposite and continue along edge of field to second stile and ditch; head across field towards stile beside lone tree. Pass to right of small pit heap to slight embankment formed in 1767.

Continue on the same line to stile on by-road, crossing fields diagonally. (The footpath may be ploughed over at certain times of the year). Near here, at the Dolly Pit, Stephenson was a brakesman. Turn right down road to cottages, then take left branch over stream to Butterlaw and on to reach your outward route at Whorlton Hall.

This walk can be extended from Hagg Bank to Prudhoe Castle (which will add a further 2 $^1/_2$ miles), or to Thomas Bewick's Birthplace Museum, which commemorates the work of the famous Tyneside wood engraver. The latter will add five miles to the original walk.

South Gosforth to Palmersville

9 miles
A walk of contrasts starting in suburban
Newcastle, continuing through park and woodland
to Dial Cottage in Killingworth, once home to the
family of railway pioneer George Stephenson.

FROM South Gosforth station turn right down Station Road. Turn left up Commercial Road and cross to Ridgewood Gardens into Hunters Road. You have crossed the site of the Jubilee Colliery.

A great ball was held by candle-light, 1,100 feet below the surface at the foot of the shaft to celebrate its sinking. Miners' families mixed with those of the promoters and surrounding gentry — obviously no safety considerations then! Unfortunately, the 90 Fathom Dyke — a geological fault — passed close by and it was impossible to locate the coal seams beyond.

Cross Metro by footbridge and con-

Dial Cottage

tinue along by road on left of stream, with Salter's Bridge on your right.*(See page 125)* At end of houses, cross stream by bridge and continue along lane, crossing golf course. Past Heathery Lane on right, take left turn along side of small stream; then bear right. Keep Low Gosforth Home Farm to your right.

Bear left once more, crossing the Ouseburn by the club-house to reach the Great North Road by Broadway East. Turn right up the dual carriageway, re-crossing the Ouseburn via the Three Mile Bridge. The road is pleasantly wooded, the east carriageway having been built within the park. Pass Northern Rugby Club to entrance of Melton Park estate. The Northumberland County Records Office is nearby.

Keep the Gosforth Park wall on your right, while the main road swings away to the left. After $\frac{1}{4}$ mile enter park by main gate; another golf club-house is on the right. Continue along drive, taking branch path to right of road, to the race course. On your right are the grandstand, exhibition hall and the other main buildings which dominate Gosforth House — the home of the Brandling family on whose estate the racecourse was established in 1882. On your left are the stables and jockeys' quarters. Pass to the left of these, into a wood. Follow ash road which, after a while, bends right to converted farm buildings.

Exit into main road on left by path; turn right along it and re-enter park by

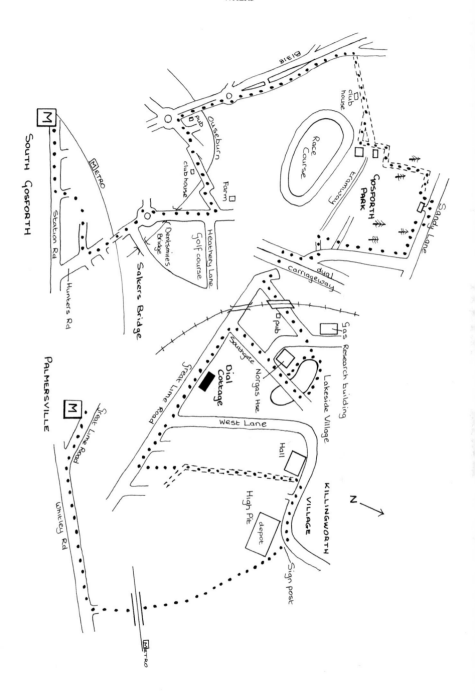

gate beyond houses. Follow footpath to left by roadside plantation to north-east corner of park. Turn right and continue by woodland paths, cross track of the 1920s tramway, to regain main drive just inside park gates.

In the 1920s a light railway was constructed through the park as a scenic route and to carry people attending the races. It connected by the Great North Road with the Gosforth tramway.

There were more than 40 tram routes in Newcastle by the 1890s using around 300 horses. The system was electrified at the turn of the century. *(See page 24)*

On leaving park, turn right and cross dual carriageway where houses commence on the other side. A footpath leads into a stretch of old road between houses. At road junction turn left to Killingworth level-crossing, site of the Racecourse station which used to be on the Edinburgh to Newcastle main line. At next junction, cross road and take footpath through shrubberies to lake. On the right shore is the British Gas headquarters building. On the left is the "Lakeside Village". (The research building which has been greatly praised is up the road from the junction on the left.) Follow shore to road across far end of lake, turn right along this into Great Lime Road.

Turn left to Dial Cottage. It was here that George Stephenson came in 1804,to work as a brakesman, and where his first wife died. The sundial, dated 1816, was made by George and his son Robert.

Continue past estate roads to signposted footpath on left. It skirts the grounds of the old hall and comes into Killingworth village — a pleasant main street with several 18th and 19th century houses. Follow this street to right and continue along West Lane to small car park on right where a pit winding wheel is displayed. This marks the site of the Killingworth High Pit where Stephenson sorted out a number of prob-lems with a Smeaton pump which had hitherto proved unable to lift the water out of the new sinking.

After this he was promoted to enginewright and given charge of all machinery in the Grand Allies *(see page 8)* collieries with £100 a year, a horse and the right to work for other proprietors, provided he kept his employers' equipment in good order!

Follow road to next corner and, beyond army depot, take signposted footpath across Killingworth Moor (way-marked) to Benton Square. Cross BR and Metro with care using stiles. Turn right through Benton Square industrial estate to Great Lime Road. Turn right to Palmersville station.

South Gosforth to Hadrian Road

7 miles
The pits around which so much of outer
Newcastle developed have now gone. This walk
however allows you to retrace the route of one of
the city's oldest wagonways which used to carry
coal from East Kenton, Fawdon and Coxlodge
pits to the river at Wallsend.

LEAVE South Gosforth station by ramp (crossing footbridge if arriving from coast or Kenton Bank Foot). At head of ramp turn left along back lane to follow west side of Metro to Stoneyhurst Road bridge. Cross Metro and continue along Stoneyhurst Road to Dene Grove on your right, turn along this to fork. Go down left fork, Dene Crescent, to Haddrick's Mill Road, turn right, and at far end of single storey terrace turn left to Ouseburn with Little Burn on your right.

Turn left along Ouseburn to metal bridge and cross, turn left and follow burn to exit on Freeman Road — cross and go up Lilburn Gardens to Coxlodge Wagonway which used to carry coals down to the Tyne. Gosforth, like most areas of Newcastle, was once a mining area. It had two working pits — the Regent and the Jubilee. Nothing remains of these now.

Turn right along the old wagonway, which has been followed in turn by horse drawn wagons, steam trains and electric trams.

There used to be a convent behind the fence on your left and beyond it was an old mining village of which only the little Methodist chapel remains — now a small garage on Benton Park Road beside the technical school.

Past the DSS office complex, cross Benton Road at "Tyneside Crossing", the point where green Tyneside trams using the wagonway crossed the yellow Newcastle trams on the main road.

Continue to Coach Lane at Bank Head — site of a cable haulage engine where the wagonway made a sharp turn south east to Bigges Main pit and the river. Turn left up Coach Lane to small new housing estate on right. Enter estate keeping to left to reach far north east corner where there is a small playground.

Follow narrow footpath by ditch, pass signposted footpath on left at far side of old barrage balloon base to reach cart track on another old wagonway. Turn left up this (you are now leaving Newcastle and entering North Tyneside).

Past playing field, turn right along lane over railway to East Benton Farm. Cross Station Road (A186) and continue for about $\frac{1}{4}$ mile to footpath to the north of houses. Turn left up this for about 700 yards then turn right down track to Rising Sun Farm.

Just south of this was the mine of the same name, closed in 1967. In the 1930s its pit head buildings won a major architectural award.

At the farm, turn left and in a short distance reach the Killingworth wagonway and turn right along it. Just before the houses, go down steps to right and follow footpath with arable land on right and the tiny Wallsend Dene on left. At signpost head down little grassy valley

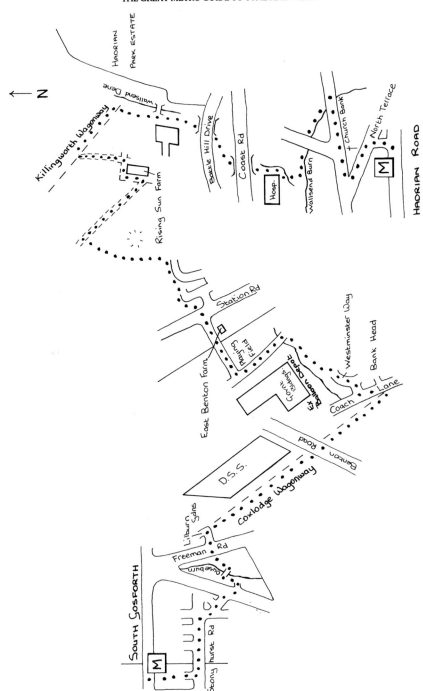

between houses keeping to right bank past footbridge. Cross Battle Hill Drive at or to right of subway and continue to subway under the Coast Road. Take footpath on left of hospital buildings and continue down dene passing under high road bridge to main road. The valley used to be crossed by a fine timber trestle wagonway bridge, unfortunately demolished some 40 years ago.

Turn right and climb hill via Church Bank to St Peter's Church, then follow church yard wall round to left then take right fork to Hadrian Road station.

Newcastle Moors & Parks to Jesmond

5 ½ miles
*A chance to appreciate the extensive stretch of undeveloped grazing
land and parkland which lies near the heart of Newcastle.*

LEAVING Ilford Road station turn left if from city, right if from Kenton Bank Foot or coast, to Moorfield railway bridge. Turn right along Moorfield keeping houses on right and Moor (here allotments) on left. Cross Moor Road South to pedestrian lights. Cross the old Great North Road at Newcastle/ Gosforth boundary (pre-1974). This used to be formed by a stream, now culverted, which was crossed, prior to the late 1920s, by the Little Bridge — a single arch two lane structure. As the bridge was unsuitable for heavy traffic there was a ford on its west side. The place was also a favourite watering hole for steam-powered lorries. The road here was frequently closed by flooding.

Turn right over the site of the ford and enter the Duke's Moor occupied in the Great War by a tented aircraft factory. The cows which wander on the Moors are those exercising the Freemen's rights of herbage.

Follow the stone wall, the old City boundary, and the park wall of Coxlodge Hall — a large mansion, now demolished, although its fine stable block still remains.

Exit on to Grandstand Road (on your left) and turn right to traffic lights. The building on your right was part of the grandstand and stables when the Newcastle Races were held on the old course prior to 1882.

Cross Kenton Road and enter the Nun's Moor. Follow right hand (stream) edge of moor about ½ mile before turning left, heading for the highest ground

but keeping golf course (dating from 1891) fence on your right. Cross Grandstand Road at about its highest point, Cow Hill, site of an old cattle and horse market. It was also where 50,000 people demonstrated against the defeat in the House of Lords, of Earl Grey's 1832 Reform Bill — a bill which was eventually passed.

Enter wooded area and climb to summit for view of surroundings. The Metro is to be thanked for much of this hill as it was raised with materials from the tunnelling as well as from work on the adjacent motorway. The hill is now a popular recreation spot used for skiing, tobogganing and by model aircraft enthusiasts. At an earlier time there were real aeroplanes on the Moor — at the Royal Flying Corps station and Armstrong Whitworth testing drome. Later it was a staging point for the King's Cup air races.

Pass over the hill and head for the Civic Centre tower crowned by a campanile. A dual carriageway should be on your right. Some ¼ mile on, cross this road by bridge and head along Hunter's Road, noticing how the Moor has been encroached upon on both sides. Land further out of town has been acquired to make up the acreage. *(See page 45)* The pleasant little streets on your left mark the old mining settlement of Spital Tongues. An underground railway carried coals from a mine which stood opposite the hospital to staithes at the mouth of the Ouseburn by way of the Victoria Tunnel. During the last war,

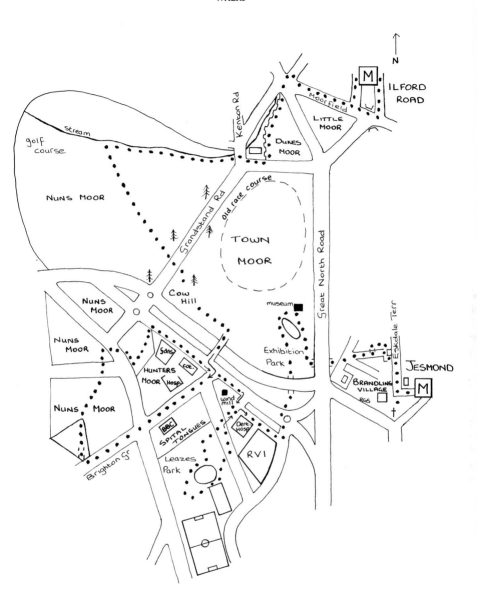

this was used as an air-raid shelter, reached via the Hancock Museum, City Baths and other points.

Pass the BBC's new buildings, known to occupants as the "Pink Palace", cross the Ponteland Road (Barrack Road) and

continue up Brighton Grove to enter Nun's Moor Park on right. Leave by far right corner, cross Fenham Hall Drive and follow footpath back to the Ponteland Road. Cross and enter (to right) Hunter's Moor. Cross this turning right down Claremont Road. The trees along most of the roads crossing the Moor were the products of a 19th century unemployment relief scheme.

On your right are the University Botanical Gardens and, beyond Hunters Road, the last remaining recognisable windmill in the town (alas without sails). About 150 yards past St Luke's church, turn right and follow footpath between Dental Hospital on left and halls of residence on right. Cross Richardson Road to Leazes Park and circuit the lake. From the high ground near the terrace, and beyond the fine early Grainger terraces, you can see the new stands of St James Park, the football ground established originally on a town moor intake and home to Newcastle United, formed in 1892 when local teams merged.

Leave the park and return to the footpath past the Dental Hospital. Turn right down the narrow road behind the Dental Hospital past pleasant terrace houses with long gardens. Thirty years ago these extended to Barras Bridge but have been gradually replaced by University buildings. The Medical School is on the right and beyond it the Royal Victoria Infirmary. Coming out on to Queen Victoria Road turn left to the roundabout, cross and enter the Exhibition Park, venue of the 1929 North East Coast Exhibition and previously known as the Bull Park — created in Queen Victoria's reign for a previous exhibition from which only the bandstand remains.

In the park, walk around the left side of the lake which was once a main source of the city's water, to the Military Vehicles Museum (open daily) situated in what was the Palace of Art in the 1929 exhibition. Adjacent to the Museum is the famous *Turbinia*, Charles Parson's experimental steam turbine craft. A replica of the old Tyne Bridge, complete with houses was erected across the lake for the 1877 exhibition. *(See page 46)*

From the museum bear left to reach subway under the Great North Road, leading into Brandling Park, much curtailed by road-building. Cross the park to the top of Lambton Road and take footpath on its left side (Brandling Place — its houses described when new as "pleasure abodes for the affluent"). Walk past pleasant terrace houses to a narrow alley passing under one of them which leads you into Brandling village. Most of the village, which was built in 1820 and included housing for workers in the local coal mines, was demolished in the 1930s. A factory and car parks now, unfortunately, replace the core, but the surrounding little streets of what used to be working-class houses are pleasant enough. Today, the village shops are mostly dress or antique establishments.

Along the east side of the village runs Eskdale Terrace, follow it to the right passing the Girls Central High School (1900) on your left and the Boys Royal Grammar School (1906) on your right. Note in front of the latter, two columns from the Virgin Mary Hospital where the school was housed from 1600 to 1844. At the end of the street is Dobson's Jesmond Parish Church of 1861. *(See page 48)* Jesmond Metro is on your left. Note the *Garden Front* sculpture outside the station. *(See page 26)*

The Ouseburn Valley

5 miles (approx)

A walk through some of the country's finest inner-city parkland, which can be extended to take in the internationally-acclaimed Byker Wall housing development. The walk can be started at either South Gosforth or West Jesmond. For instructions from the latter see page 128.

Jesmond Dene

LEAVE South Gosforth Metro station by incline (first crossing footbridge if coming from Kenton Bank Foot or coast). Cross main road to examine St Nicholas' church, parish church of Gosforth when the area was mainly country houses interspersed with small mining settlements. There has been a church here since the 12th century at least, although the present church dates from the beginning of the last century; it's a pleasing little building with a short octagonal steeple.

From the church follow the main road (A191) over the Metro and down Station Road. Halfway down the hill, turn left up to field; cross to Ridgewood Gardens and into Hunter's Road, and recross Metro by footbridge. A short distance ahead is Salters Bridge, which should be

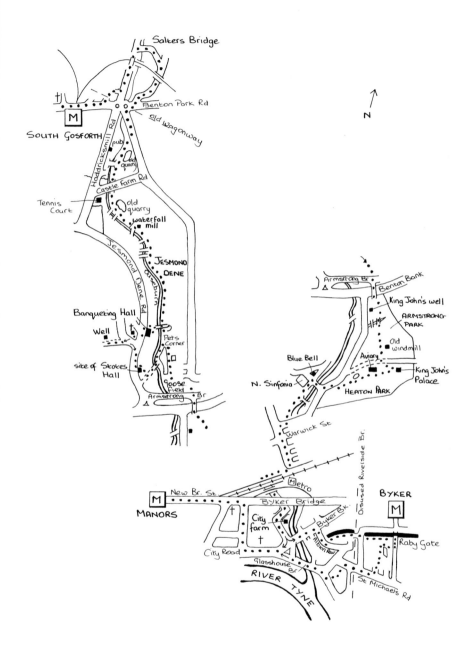

examined underneath to identify the ribbed part of one arch, which reveals its ancient origin. The bridge once carried packhorse traffic between the coastal salt-pans and the monastic settlements of the upper Tyne valley.

After crossing the bridge follow the road to Salters Lane (A189) and turn right, passing back under the Metro. Continue to double roundabout close to Victory Inn. At this point the Coxlodge wagonway (See page 105) crossed the valley on a high trestle bridge. This wagonway was an early mineral line constructed with timber plates before the introduction of iron rails and flanged wheels.

Cross the main roads and strike up the rise opposite, signposted "High Heaton". Past bungalows on right enter the most recent and most northerly section of Jesmond Dene and follow the path downstream.

Above the other bank the Millstone pub, and the name of the road beyond it, recall Haddrick's flint mill which once stood on this site. The last visible trace was the mill-race, and that has now been filled in. Beyond the metal quarry bridge a small weir locates a stream entering through the far bank. This is the Little Burn which, until 1974, divided Newcastle from Gosforth — its fiercely independent northern neighbour.

The area from this point to the Castle Farm Bridge used to be part of the garden of Crag Hall, the long stone house opposite, which was formed from a row of workers' cottages. In season there is still an attractive show of rhododendrons.

A narrow tunnel through the abutment of the graceful high-arched bridge has been re-opened to make a way into the next stretch of valley, which was previously attached to Jesmond Dene House. Here the valley becomes wider and several paths follow it, a 1930s bridge joining those on opposite sides.

On the west side, beyond the public park, a level area contains the nursery gardens and a large brick building, inside which is one of the country's few remaining Real Tennis courts. This ancient game, still played today, is a form of tennis played indoors within a four walled court. King Henry VIII was said to be very good at it.

The next bridge is the first of those forming part of the original Dene given to the city 100 years ago by Sir William Armstrong. He lived on the high ground to the south; just below it are some stepping stones — the first of the many decorative features Sir William was to introduce. The most spectacular — the main waterfall — can be seen by following the path down the left of the valley to the next bridge. Heavy rain will fill out the adjacent falls.

At the end of the bridge are the ruins of the 14th century over-shot water flint mill and cottage, which featured in many 19th century paintings. Pass along the ledge at the side of the mill, past the next fall and a Rococo bridge, to a pair of bridges side by side. The first bridge, bore Armstrong's carriage-way, while the second provided public access up the valley. This road was fenced, a footbridge over it connected the two west banks of the Dene; parts of the stone supports can still be seen.

The next bridge spans both road and stream; at the far side of it climb the steps to bridge level. On your right is the dry race which served the Busy Mills. Turn left over bridge and climb to ruins of John Dobson's banqueting hall, a sad remnant of a once-attractive structure in which Armstrong installed an hydraulic organ. Turn away, then climb to left. The preserved building is Norman Shaw's fore buildings to the earlier hall. (See page 45)

Cross Jesmond Dene Road to the ruins of St Mary's Chapel, above a little wooded side-valley. Once a place of pilgrimage, the medieval chapel dates back to, at least, the 13th century. Nearby is St Mary's Well where miracles, including the appearance of Jesus, are said to have taken place. To see what remains of it, enter the lane leading up the tiny side-valley between stone piers. The "remains" are on your right some 50 yards up the lane. These are not so ancient, as a local owner converted the well to a bathing place in 1827.

A shorter alternative to this walk can be taken from West Jesmond station to join it at this point.

After leaving the station, go down Sunbury Avenue to St Georges Terrace, turning left on to Osborne Road and across to St George's Church — probably the city's finest Victorian suburban church. Continue south along Osborne Road past Lindisfarne Road and Reid Park Road junction to a footpath on your left which leads to The Grove. Follow this down to St Mary's Well.

Return to Jesmond Dene Road and walk to the right. Where the footpath crosses a small green was the site of an interesting Elizabethan house, called Stote's Hall after its historic owner. The hall was damaged by bombing during the war and demolished in 1953. Turn left down the steep footpath, pleasant in cherry blossom time, to a little footbridge.

Follow the stream up where it is dammed to provide a home for swans which nest on the west, inaccessible, bank. In front of you as you pass Busy Cottages you may see an archway in the bank of the stream. This was the outfall from the large mill which once stood here. In the garden beyond is the sluice which controlled the flow. There also used to be an iron foundry and hamlet here once.

Turn right down the valley road; on your right is Pets Corner which houses a collection of small animals and exotic birds. The Dene Information Centre is nearby. Continue down the road past the large field on your right, this is the old goose field — until the last war it was full of honking geese, as hundreds of birds were fattened up for the festive season. The field is now laid out with flowers, shrubs and a pets' cemetery.

Ahead is Armstrong Bridge — the high iron viaduct which Sir William Armstrong built across the Dene. According to local legend this was at his wife's behest to save horses the long pull up Benton Bank. Restoration work proceeds whenever funds are available. An arts and crafts fair is held on the bridge every Sunday morning in the summer and before Christmas.

Before reaching the main road turn left up the valley side, then bear right to the gates on the eastern bridge abutment. Turn left and then pass through broken iron gates to enter Armstrong Park across another iron bridge spanning Benton Bank. Look for the stump of a windmill on your left as you walk along this section. The so-called Well of King John is further down the hillside by a lower path. The grassy area which appears on your right just before leaving the park used to be occupied by a tea pavilion, to which guests of Lord Armstrong would have been driven on an afternoon's outing.

Follow the path to Jesmond Vale Lane and enter Heaton Park on the other side. The new terraced building on your right is a reconstruction of the old aviary.

To your left is a path leading to the ruins of a 13th century fortified house known locally as "King John's Palace" because the king stayed there in the mid-13th century. The two-storeyed dwelling belonged to Adam de Gesemuth (Jesmond), a wealthy baron and Sheriff of Northumberland. Retrace your footsteps back to the terrace past the "aviary" then veer right down the dip in the ground, keeping the children's play

Byker Wall estate

area on your left — note how the land rises to a pleasant belt of trees.

On the right is a disused paddling pool, once the site of an old bear pit. Exit through door in wall, onto the valley road. To your right, by the Green Waters footbridge, are the remains of another dam. Go left instead, to the Blue Bell Bridge and cross into what used to be a three-pub hamlet but which now comprises nothing older than the Blue Bell Inn and a pleasant double-fronted house. The village was originally the home of local pit and quarry workers.

Turn left between the stream and the Northern Sinfonia rehearsal rooms — a small water mill and demonstration saw mill may be built near here in the future. Continue to the point where the stream enters a large culvert. This conveys the stream under a huge refuse tip, formed in this section of the valley earlier this century. The culvert was used as an air-raid shelter during the last war. Take the path over the culvert into the side street; turn right, then left, and cross Warwick Street. Go straight ahead with ends of terraced streets to your left and playing fields to the right.

In front of you is a fine viaduct which carries the main Edinburgh railway. Turn right down path to pass under viaduct to a small stone bridge; the other end of the culvert is to your right. Overhead, the new concrete bridge carries the Metro. Its neighbour, the Byker road-bridge, made possible the development of the eastern suburbs; in front of you is the city farm.

Continue along Lime Street, keeping the Ouseburn on your left; here it is tidal and used as club moorings — although a more "upmarket" marina development is threatened at the time of writing). From Ouseburn bridge you can visit the Byker Wall and the "village" it protects. *(See below)*

Otherwise, turn right up Cut Bank

into City Road coming off Glasshouse bridge. The mound on your left is an old ballast hill; beneath you is the Victoria Tunnel. This underground railway used to carry coals from a mine in Spital Tongues to a staithe at this point. Along City Road to your right is St Ann's church, once part of the affluent suburb of Stepney. This is a pleasant little church of 1682. Just past it make your way northward up Crawhall Road to St Dominics on New Bridge Street. Follow the street to the left to reach Manors station — the new Metro station rather than the large, half-demolished station on the BR main line. The shop fronts along New Bridge Street disguise pleasant terraces. A new multi-screen cinema is on your right.

BYKER DETOUR *(approx. 1 mile)*

To reach this interesting and pioneering housing project, leave Lime Street by the bridge over the Ouseburn and climb Byker Bank (scrap-yard on right). Turn right along Albion Row round the scrap-yard. Just past the entrance to Shepherd's on your right, leave Albion Row to the left at notice board with map of district.

Take right-hand path under pergola into the village and walk up the inside of the "wall", crossing the cutting of the disused Riverside branch. Opposite the little shop in the wall, turn right along Clive Walk to a small square. Bear left and follow Shipley Walk to the Raby Gate, where a way through the wall leads to the Byker Metro station. From the gate go straight forward for a short distance, before turning right for Norfolk Square. Beyond the square turn left down Brinkburn Walk and on to Brinkburn Square. Pass to the left of the Chevron by Dibley Street to reach St Michael's Road, leaving the village.

Turn right to cross the railway cutting once more, then left into St Lawrence Square. Cross the park into Walker Road.

Once more turn right to cross Glasshouse bridge, a long, high-level, arched structure which spans the Ouseburn near its mouth. The structure on the right, with the elaborate towers, was once the local school. At the top of Cut Bank resume the main route.

Benton to Palmersville

3 miles

*A short walk around the old Killingworth wagonway with
many points of interest for those interested in natural history.*

LEAVE Benton station on north side (ie trains from city) and take footpath alongside the Metro across main road, continuing through subway and across bridge over main railway line. Drop to ground level and continue along north side of Metro by North Croft and footpath. At end of Ashcroft Drive turn right through subways to field path with Procter and Gamble's research buildings on right. Turn left along the old Coast Road, A191, to roundabout at Station Road.

At far side enter bridleway to right of filling station and follow plantation to Killingworth wagonway. Turn right down this until you reach wood on right then turn on to woodland path. Make anti-clockwise circuit of hill following tracks to rejoin wagonway. On the other side of this is the Swallow Pond nature reserve.

Pass along left side of pond using stiles and paths provided — several wetland projects are in progress. Continue on path, with trotting track on left, to Scaffold Hill where an old hospital contains The Rising Sun Resource Centre where there is an exhibition open to the public.

Leaving resource centre turn left (south) down the lane then turn left again on footpath alongside grounds for 300 yards to Scaffold Hill Farm. Turn left at farm and follow farm road north but where it swings left continue straight on along field path towards the Wheatsheaf Inn. Cross road at roundabout and go along Great Lime Road to Palmersville Metro.

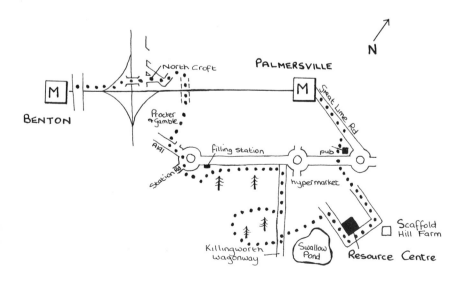

Hadrian Road to Wallsend

2 miles
An historic trip along an old Roman road to the town
which started life as a fortress at the end of Hadrian's Wall
and became one of the world's leading shipbuilding centres.

LEAVE Hadrian Road Metro station to north (if coming from coast, crossing the Metro). Bear left along North Terrace to St Peters church, set in a large walled churchyard in which are buried the bodies of many of the 102 miners killed in a local mine explosion of 1835. Notice, incidentally, how many pubs in the area are named after mines — such as New Winning and Rising Sun.

The church was built in 1809 to replace the old Holy Cross church (*see below*). Note the set of stocks by the west door. From church, descend hill (to right) to Wallsend Dene; at the road the dene discharges into a channel known as the Willington Gut. There used to be an extensive 18th century ropeworks on the left bank of the channel. The building with the curved roof is the old Willington Mill of 1801. Beyond it, on either side of the gut, are shipyards devoted to off-shore oil-rigs and platforms. Looking up, you will see a fine viaduct which still carries the Metro over the little valley; previously it bore the Tynemouth railway which was electrified in 1904.

Cross the road and follow the paved track up the far bank of the dene, passing under high bridge. After a short distance strike up the grass diagonally to reach the fenced enclosure containing the ruins of the old Holy Cross Church, which consist of the lower walls of a very small mid-12th century nave and chancel, and of a 17th century south porch.

Many of the gravestones have either an artistic or an historical interest. There are several 17th and 18th century memorials to members of the Henzell family, who brought their glass-making skills from Alsace and Lorraine. These skills still live on in the district, as does the family. Many other memorials were apparently taken for bake stones.

Return to the paved track at the site of Stephenson's timber viaduct, demolished relatively recently. Follow the track up the valley, to cross the stream and enter the green by a narrow road. Ponder a while on why the church and the old village were built on opposite sides! The hospital incorporates parts of the

Willington Gut

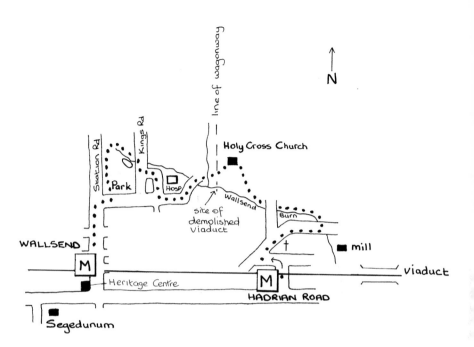

17th century hall. In spite of its Roman origins, Wallsend is mostly a recent town, owing its existence first to mining and then to shipbuilding. Most of the buildings are 19th century; miners' streets such as Rochdale Street of 1868, named after the Co-operative pioneers, reflect the attitudes of the period. The town achieved borough status in 1900, but lost it in 1974.

From the Green turn north up Lily Bank, across King's Road to Richardson Dees Park on left, Hall gardens on right. When the end of the Roman wall was demolished to enlarge a shipyard, it was reassembled in the park. Bearing left in the park, exit past the greenhouses into North Road. Turn right into Station Road which will lead you (left) to Wallsend Metro station. At this point — before you go down Station Road — you may want to visit the Buddle Arts

Centre at number 258b (open Tuesday to Saturday).

Continue under the Metro to Buddle Street and, on the corner, the Heritage Centre where a pictorial history of Wallsend is displayed alongside other exhibits. Immediately to the west, Buddle Street crosses the site of the Roman fort of *Segedunum*, the most easterly on the Roman Wall. *(See page 27)* In the grassy area south of the road you can see the remains of the headquarters which have been left exposed following back-filling of the rest of the excavations.

North of the road the line of a barrack street has been marked out with paving. The relics were lucky to have survived as a mine was sunk just outside the walls. This was later the scene, in 1821, of an explosion which killed 52 men and boys.

Percy Main to Railway Museum

$1\frac{1}{2}$ miles

A "railway walk" along the path of an old colliery line to the Stephenson Railway Museum. The walk can be continued to either Shiremoor or West Monkseaton.

"Killingworth Billy", one of Stephenson's first locomotives, on display at the Museum.

LEAVING Percy Main station turn northwards (if coming from coast, pass first under Metro bridge); the Percy Arms Hotel should be on your left. The track of the old Backworth Colliery railway has been relaid and it is intended that steam trains will run between Percy Main and the Stephenson Railway museum. One and a half miles of track have been laid and the line should open in summer, 1990 — probably operating at weekends while the museum is open.

Timetables will be posted at Percy Main Metro and the museum. The terminus will be slightly west of the Metro station behind the Percy Arms.

A short distance up Station Road, bear slightly right into the grassy area and continue northwards to the right of the hedge. The footway will take you under the Wallsend-North Shields road and will then be joined, on your left, by the railway. Pass under the coast road (A1058) and continue to Middle Engine Lane; the railway museum entrance is on your left.

The museum, open Tuesdays to Sundays from late April to late September, houses a collection of locomotives and rolling stock of various periods. These include an early Stephenson loco from the nearby Killingworth railway and a streamlined Gresley Pacific used to draw the Silver Jubilee non-stop to King's Cross.

Leaving the museum, turn right along Middle Engine Lane and take either of these two routes...

a) Continue into New York, crossing Norham Road and going straight ahead over the by-pass and the village main street to follow Murton Lane into Murton village. Carry straight on, passing the 1930s council houses to your right. Follow signposted field path to crossing over Metro. Bear right to paved path between houses. At street turn right, left and right again to follow residential street to West Monkseaton station.

b) Leave lane at the old railway bed and continue northwards along the bed to the New York-West Allotment Road. At nearby roundabout to right, take Park Lane (left) to Shiremoor station.

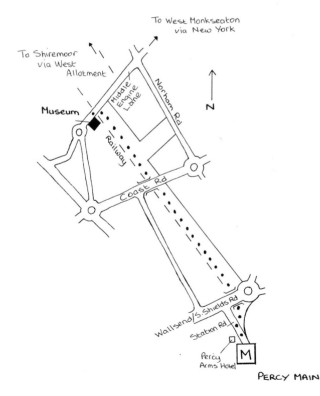

WALKS
SOUTH OF THE TYNE

The Derwent Valley

16¹/₂ miles

*A chance to explore one of the area's most secluded
and heavily-wooded valleys, once the cradle of the
local ironworking industry.*

WHEN the 1990 National Garden Festival closes, it will eventually be possible to combine this walk with the Gateshead town trail which will enable you to follow the side of the Tyne and its tributary from the town centre into deep countryside. You will also be able to extend it even further up the Derwent Valley and up the Derwent Gorge and past the reservoir to Blanchland, connecting with any of the adjacent valleys of the Wear, East Allen or Devil's Water.

Start this walk from the Gateshead Metro Centre station on the Newcastle-Carlisle line (BR), named after the shopping centre and not associated with the Tyneside Metro system! The only way out of the station is through the shopping complex — by way of a bridge which takes you into the upper level. The Metro Centre is claimed to be Europe's largest shopping and leisure complex, attracting more than 20 million people in 1989. There are some 350 shops on three miles of covered malls, some of which are distinguished by "themes" — the Roman Forum, the Antique Village, the Mediterranean Village, the Garden Court, etc. There is a ten screen cinema, 28 lane superbowl, a "landscaped" indoor fairground, a creche and some 50 pubs, cafes and other eating places.

Should you wish to explore, the Centre is designated in quadrants of yellow (north west), blue (north east), green (south east) and red (south west), each with adjacent car parks with matching indicators. Location plans are posted at most mall intersections and directory leaflets are available. A short tour of most of the features can be made at the upper level.

Leave the station bridge, turn right and circle the main malls (roughly a figure of eight layout) in an anti-clockwise direction, that is, turning right outside C & A but left at the next intersection (unless you wish to visit the fairground) into the Mediterranean Village. Left again in the red sector and half right into the green at the far end of which an escalator will take you down to Marks & Spencer.

For those wanting to leave the centre at the first opportunity, turn left after leaving the bridge to pass through the Antiques Village and Roman Forum then left at Hennes to reach the escalator outside Marks & Spencer. Cross Marks & Spencer to exit into green car park then turn left to the last parking aisle (No. 25) which leads to a road intersection.

Cross the main distributor road straight ahead into minor road (to Dunston) with RCI factory on left. Turn right up strip of grass to right of Frazer Plant and up the outside of the Federation Brewery fence. This was Cross Lane and it leads to a tunnel under the bypass. About 100 yards beyond the tunnel, take path to right along edge of field to reach Market Lane. Turn right then left opposite Fire Station along Clavering Road and down to Swalwell Bank until you reach the entrance to the Derwent Walk. You won't be able to miss this as it is marked by a train sculpture, *(See page 60)* echoing the great railway heritage of the valley.

The next three miles are straight forward, following the bed of the old Consett railway track lifted in 1962. The first stretch of valley has only recently been recovered from a large cokeworks — the last remnants may still be visible.

After about one and a quarter miles, you will see across the valley five streets of small houses climbing up the hillside between woods. Watch for a path passing below you under a small bridge and crossing the river by a footbridge. From here a slight diversion can be made to the left by a minor path which leads up to the ruins of a fortified medieval manor house, Old Hollinside. In 1730 it became part of the Gibside Estate and was abandoned. The path then continues down the slope to regain the railway bed.

You should be back on the main route to cross the first of the viaducts which carry it from side to side of the river which from here onwards winds and loops, sometimes cutting into the woods to form high cliffs. In those woods to your right just off the Lockhaugh road is the Country Park Visitor Centre. As you enter more open country and the river becomes more distant, look left across the haughs to the woods of Gibside. In amongst them is the creamy shell of the mansion built early in the 17th century by the Blakistons of Coxhoe on an estate acquired a century earlier by marriage into the locally famous Marley family.

As in so many local families, the male line died out and the heiress took the estate with her when she married one of the Bowes family of Streatlam Castle, near Barnard Castle. Her grand-daughter heiress similarly married John Lyon, Earl of Strathmore, and they joined their names as Bowes-Lyon. It is this background which brings the Queen Mother (Elizabeth Bowes-Lyon) on visits to Gibside — the chapel is said to be a favourite of hers.

At Rowlands Gill, the site of the sta-

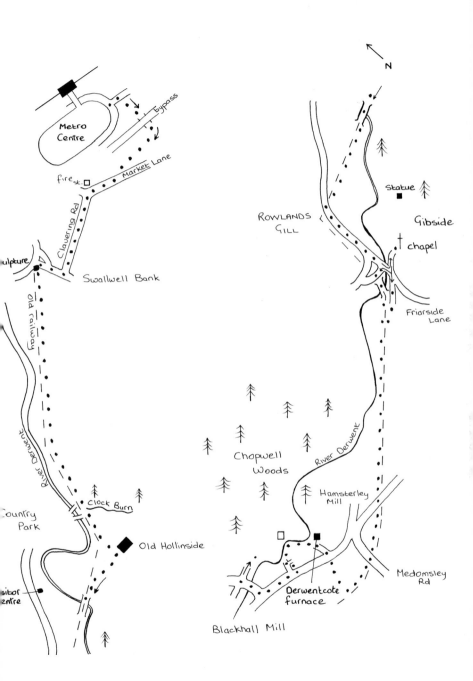

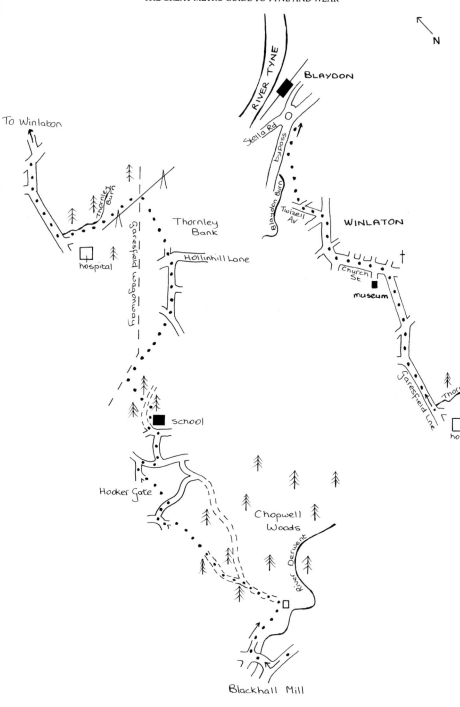

tion and adjacent lengths of track have been developed and you will emerge on the main valley road, the A694; turn left down it, branching left again towards the river on the Burnopfield road. Just over the bridge, turn left into the entrance to Gibside, leading you to the Chapel which was given to the National Trust in 1965. During the summer it is open Wednesday, Saturday and Sunday afternoons. The Trust holds an annual service in June but accommodation is very limited.

The chapel was commissioned by George Bowes and work on it started in 1760 to a design by James Paine. Bowes died, however, in the same year and the property passed to the heiress, the Countess of Strathmore. She eventually married an adventurer from Ireland and building work was not resumed until the next generation. Consecrated in 1812, the chapel was 72 years in the making. The story of the Irish husband's flight round the country from the law, taking his wife with him in an almost non-stop carriage ride, is a fascinating one which can be followed in *The Unhappy Countess* by R. Arnold.

The chapel design, like that of several buildings in the country, is loosely based on that of a villa near Vicenza by Palladio. It is cruciform in plan with a dome over the crossing — common in the Eastern Mediterranean but not so in England until recently when centrally-placed altars have become more popular. There is an attractive three-decked pulpit and box pews are situated in the corners — those of the family are cushioned! From the portico stretches a long avenue of mature Turkish oaks, which leads to a 140 foot high column bearing the statue of British Liberty.

Built in 1757, this is probably the highest columned monument in the country, exceeding Grey's monument in Newcastle and that of Nelson in Trafalgar Square. Scattered round the avenue,

and not all visible from it, are the ruins of the mansion, the stables and the orangery, unoccupied since the first world war. Trust ownership extends only to the avenue and chapel, however, so the other buildings are out of bounds. However, access to much of the woodland has been under negotiation and by the time of your visit walks through it may have been opened.

Return to the Burnopfield road, on which a farm is sometimes open to visitors. To regain the railway track, cross the road from the Gibside drive and follow the Friarside Lane opposite. If you want to see the second of the great viaducts, return across the road bridge and climb to your left. After a short distance along the track you will see the remains of the chapel of a 12th century friary attached to the farm on your right.

The next three miles are through deep cuttings and over further high (up to 120 foot) viaducts. The trees which have been enclosing you eventually drop away and soon you will be gazing down on their tops far below. The only intrusions are the railway houses at Lintz Green station and the fringe of a housing estate at Hamsterley Mill. Just past the latter the track is broken by the Medomsley road. A quarter of a mile beyond this, look for a path on your right which will lead you down to the main road. Cross this and go down the lane opposite, on right of house (by "no cars" notice).

On the right is a strange-looking stone structure, conical in shape. This is the Derwentcote cementation furnace, dating back to the days when iron was produced in wooded areas using charcoal in lieu of coke. When the furnace ceased making wrought iron over 100 years ago, it was already a century-and-a-half out of date. Wrought iron is no longer produced having been replaced by steel, but its rust resistance made it a superior material for gates and other decorative exterior metalwork. The furnace is being restored by English Heritage.

Near the foot of the lane, bearing left, take a footpath over a stile to follow the south bank of the Derwent for about a quarter of a mile to stables. The track to your right should lead to Blackhall Mill but it is heavily used by horses in training and gets very muddy. Instead, go left up drive and along path on its left to main road.

Go right for 600 yards and turn down to Blackhall Mill bridge. In a little under half a mile along north bank of river, to your right, turn left at farm along footpath through Chopwell Woods — the largest afforested area in this locality. After a mile of forest ride, continue due north to Heavy Gate, and the Chopwell to High Spen road. Just up this road turn right along lane for 300 yards before taking footpath to left which, bearing to right, will bring you into Hooker Gate village. Turn right down main road for a short distance before turning left up School Lane. The school contains a woodcarving of the Durham Miners Gala — completed by Keith Alexander during a short-term residency at the school—another of the recent art works commissioned by Gateshead council. A quarter of a mile along the footpath on left of school (end in dip of road), bear left across Spen Banks.

An easier way is to follow the adjacent forestry road (no right of way) for a quarter of a mile to the footpath crossing point by a small stream. The footpath bears right a quarter of a mile from this crossing to join bed of old Garesfield wagonway.

You now join the Heritage Way from Wylam to Causey Arch. (See pages 8/9) Where the wagonway swings left through a cutting, leave it and follow boundary paths, keeping Sherburn Tower to your right, until you reach Hollinhill Lane. Cross this and follow left hand path, signposted Thornley Lane. Three hundred yards short of Low Thornley leave the Heritage Way, turning left on the near side of electricity grid lines. Pass through small wooded valley to reach minor road (Garesfield Lane) to right of Norman's Riding Hospital (Care village). Follow this to right under cables into Winlaton, reaching Church Street.

Winlaton Church is an attractive, tall, towered structure built in 1828 and designed by Ignatius Bonomi, designer of many churches in County Durham around that time. There is also an attractive rectory nearby. A short distance up Church Street is the library and clinic, behind which is the cottage forge – the last of the old chain forges which, particularly in the Derwent Valley, made heavy chains for the shipbuilding and mining industries.

Continue north up Church Street and its continuation North Street, passing the bus depot. After about half a mile look for Black Lane on your left. Turn into it but take the right fork, Twizell Avenue. From this a path leads down into the valley of the Blaydon Burn leading to Stella Road, the A695 main road up the south side of the Tyne.

The new Ryton-Crawcrook bypass is being constructed along the valley and several old tracks and footpaths are being affected. A new walkway is being built along the south side of the bypass and should be usable by the time you read this. If not, continue from North Street to Blaydon Bank and down it to meet up with the walkway route at the big roundabout. Blaydon station (BR) is at the far side of the dual carriageway.

The Wear Valley

16 miles

This walk to one of the North East's most famous landmarks can be lengthened or shortened to suit individual interests.

LEAVING Sunderland BR station, turn left into Fawcett Street and then right along it to the main crossing. Cross diagonally to the museum on the corner then go up right side of museum into Mowbray Park. Continue southwards through park to the middle where a bridge crosses a deep railway cutting (old branch to Hudson Docks). Bear right to footbridge over Burdon Road into the Civic Centre. Bear right again through main court and exit to Park Lane Bridge over the old railway. Turn left along near side of cutting down Cowan Terrace.

Cross Stockton Road into Princess Alice Street. You are now entering an area of terraces and squares which will give you an idea of what old Sunder-land used to look like. Turn left along Worcester Street, then right into Argyle Street to cross into Azalea Terrace. Take the second right into Briery Vale Road, cross Tunstall Vale then turn left into The Grove. The houses are good quality, mid-19th century, and were mainly built for the upper middle class on the site of urban mansions of the very rich, a few of which remain. It is also an area of trees and open spaces — the Ashbrooke Ground, the Backhouse and Barley Mow Parks and the grounds of several schools and other institutions.

From the Grove turn right round the church into Ashbrooke Road and follow its curves to Willow Bank Road on right. Turn right along Queen Alexandra Road (B1405) for about half a mile to the gira-

Penshaw Monument

THE GREAT METRO GUIDE TO TYNE AND WEAR

tory system where it meets Durham Road. Cross this main road (A690) to Barnes Park, just on the left of the road of that name (continuation of B1405). Once into the park, turn left up the small valley which forms the spine of a linear park some one and a half miles long. Continue up it crossing in succession Ettrick Grove, Springwell Road and Grindon Lane.

To visit the Grindon Museum (closed Thursdays) which contains period rooms and shops, turn right up this road for about 300 yards (on left opposite bus turning loop).

Back at the park, continue to Tay Road then take the footpath on the far side. This takes you to the left of Grindon Hill, following the Barnes valley to the point on the old borough boundary where housing ends but not before it has almost closed the gap beween the green valley and open country. Slightly to your right as you emerge is Hastings Hill, an archaeological site which has yielded relics now in the main museum.

Once over the old boundary* *(see below)* into the open, turn left and follow Salters' Lane down the right hand edge of the housing into Middle Herrington. Turn right along Summerhill or Hillcrest to Middle Herrington Farm where Foxcover Road bends right. Continue straight on to cross A19 and reach West Herrington. At this point a diversion can be made to a Site of Special Scientific Interest (SSSI) at old quarry workings. (Enter the hamlet at St Cuthbert's Road, bear left to the main street Fletcher Terrace). Turn right for a few yards then turn into lane on left; follow it south (right fork), keeping Herrington Hill to your left. The SSSI is a fairly narrow irregular area some 700 yards long. Return to St Cuthbert's Road and, at the end of it, turn left and follow path northwards. Bear left at plantation to left of electricity transformer.

If you are prepared to omit the SSSI

visit, some two miles can be knocked off your walk by reaching this point direct from that where you crossed the old boundary.

Follow the footpath to Hastings Hill Farm, turn left along farm road (tumulus on right) to Foxcover Road. Turn right up this to cross A19 and left down the far side of this on road to transformer. Before this leaves the A19, branch right down the plantation.

From the plantation, follow lane towards Flinton Hill Farm, turning left by the farm. On reaching the A183 turn left to Penshaw Hill House on a loop of old road and climb footpath to the monument which commemorates one of the key figures associated with the 1832 Reform Act and who also, by negotiating home rule for Canada, laid the foundations for the present British Commonwealth.

The roofless temple, now owned by the National Trust, is 100 feet long, 53 feet wide and 70 feet high with 18 columns. It was built as a double-size replica of the Temple of Theseus in the 1840s by public subscription, as a tribute to John George Lambton, the first Earl of Durham and a descendant of an earlier Lambton whose carelessness, legend has it, bred a fearsome serpent which he eventually had to slay on his return from the Crusades. There is open access to the monument — on a clear day it offers excellent views across Tyneside and Wearside.

Head left along the edge of the wood down the slope westward toward Penshaw church. Penshaw means "wooded hill", and was an ancient oak wood until the 17th century. *(A bus can be taken from the village back to Sunderland if desired.)* On reaching the main street at the foot of Hill Lane, turn right and then follow the field path down the hill. Cross the lower Cox Green by-road and abandoned railway at right angles (footpath sign "To Wear"), to a cottage near the end of the Victoria Viaduct.

This fine structure, with ten arches,

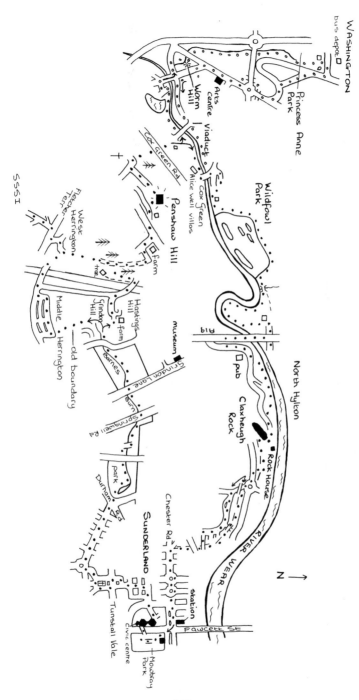

was opened in 1838 on the day of Victoria's coronation to link the Durham Junction Railway with the north and south banks of the Wear. It is now used only by diverted services, although the possibility exists that it may carry freight when the Channel tunnel opens. It rises 128 feet above the river and its main arches, when built, were claimed to be the largest in Europe. The viaduct was based on the Roman bridge at Alcantara in Spain.

Pass in front of the cottage (beware dogs and goats), swing left and then follow the woodland path down to the right. Turn right on the main valley path, downriver, though you will at first be separated from the river by the site of some old staithes. On the right of the path you can see the tunnels by which stone was brought to the staithes for loading on to keels. The riverside wood is natural mixed deciduous. Just past the first houses of Cox Green you will see Alice's Well, until recently the only water supply. The Oddfellows Arms, just past the bridge, serves bar snacks. Cross the Wear by the footbridge which has now replaced the ferry.

From the viaduct an alternative, longer route can be taken to include Washington town centre. *(This will add a further five miles to the original walk.)* Turn left along riverbank under the viaduct to the little Mount Pleasant Lake and cross river by road bridge. In front of you is Worm Hill around which reputedly coiled the famous Lambton Worm — although some say it was Penshaw Hill.

Legend has it that the mythical creature used to live by the River Wear and was fished out one day by a young member of the Lambton family who threw it contemptuously down a nearby well. While he was off fighting in the Crusades the worm grew into a fearsome creature and became so large that it could wind itself nine times around Worm Hill. On his return from the crusades, Lambton slew the worm with the help of a witch. In return he promised to kill the first living thing he met after doing the deed or else a curse would descend on the Lambton family. Unfortunately the first thing he saw was his father and he was unable to keep to his side of the bargain. As a result nine generations of Lambtons died untimely deaths.

The James Steel Park now encircles the Hill. From the riverside road to left, head up little valley to the left of Worm Hill, crossing Biddick Lane and entering, beyond Northumberland Way, the Princess Anne Park. At the head of this is the town centre with the Galleries shopping centre. *(Take a bus back to Sunderland from this point should you not wish to return on foot.)* Return through Biddick from right hand top corner of park down east side on Parkway, fork left along Titchfield Road to rejoin Parkway at North Biddick Hall. Go left to Biddick Lane and turn right down this, pass under Northumberland Way by subway and continue down to the Arts Centre which occupies tastefully converted farm buildings by the side of what used to be the Chester-le-Street to Washington railway. In addition to craft workshops and art gallery, the Centre includes a theatre and restaurant. Continue by Biddick Lane, Fallowfield Way and Worm Hill Terrace to riverside. Follow riverbank to left, repassing under viaduct to Cox Green. *This diversion will add five miles to the walk.*

Leave Cox Green bridge by taking the posted footpath behind Barmston Ferry house and follow it down river below High Barmston to the perimeter fence of The Wildfowl Park. Follow this round to the main entrance. The park is one of those operated by the Wildfowl Trust set up by Peter Scott in 1946. There are 100 acres of land sloping down to the Wear in which ponds of all sizes in a variety of habitats are designed to attract a wide range of birds.

More than 1,000 swans, ducks and geese of many species inhabit the upper ponds by the Centre building, while larger, more overgrown stretches of water nearer the river attract migratory birds. These and the wooded areas are found by many species other than waterfowl. Nearly 200 different species have been seen. The park is open daily except at Christmas. During the summer a pleasure boat runs between the park and Sunderland quayside.

Leave the car park by the exit road and turn right along the cinder track (signposted to Low Barmston, and probably muddy). At next sign (to North Hylton) turn off right over the footbridge and follow the wildfowl park perimeter fence, finally zig-zagging down steps towards the riverside. The path has a good chipped surface but with numerous steps.

At a second, larger footbridge over a stream, the path forks — the left hand path leads direct over fields to the A19 bridge over the Wear. It is uninteresting and very muddy, so it is worth taking the longer woodland path by the riverside (where you will find a fine display of celandines in spring).

Approaching the road bridge, the path climbs gradually to its level. Ignoring signs which can be rotated by idle hands, bear left into the farm and then right beyond the new-looking house. After passing under the A19 take the steps up to the road level and cross the bridge, leaving it on the far bank by the path which swings round and descends to the south bank of the river by Offerton Lane. At the riverside, by the Golden Lion, is a picnic enclosure from which a footpath continues downriver opposite North Hylton hamlet clustered round the Shipwrights pub.

In less than a mile you reach Claxheugh Rock, a great limestone cliff overlooking the river. At Rock House, near which a Roman sword was found in the river some 100 years ago, turn back up path, scaling east end of the rock to reach the track of the abandoned railway from Penshaw to Sunderland. Follow the track for half a mile to the roundabout at the west end of Pallion New Road.

From here the track runs along the south side of the road before swinging away from the river. This next half mile is to be improved at some time in the future but is meanwhile usable. If work is in progress when you visit, take Merle Terrace, the main road from the roundabout passing under the railway, to next main crossroads. Turn left along Neville Road, Shepherd Street, Thornbury Street, Robert Street and Milton Street to regain the track beyond the works.

The footpath from here to the town centre is due to be improved at some time. If work is in progress parallel road routes should not be difficult to find if the way is obstructed.

If following the railway track to return to the station — leave it between Chester Road and New Durham Road where it crosses open space. Exit to right up access track leading to Summerhill, a pleasant terrace facing a small linear park. Cross track by bridge at right hand end of terrace and pass through Sunderland Technology Park to reach The Green and Brougham Street. From this exit the railway track is in a deep cutting and there is no escape until you reach Park Lane. This is, at present, only possible by trespassing over railway sidings and should not be attempted until the footway is completed sometime in 1990.

Tyne Tunnel
to Jarrow

5 miles (4 if bus used)
A walk under the river to what was once the hub of Charles
Palmer's industrial empire plus a visit to one of the
world's most historic churches.

St Pauls

LEAVE Howdon station turning right (trains from Newcastle) down Howdon Lane towards the river; on your left is a park, on your right the gas works. Cross the course of dismantled Riverside branch into Willington Quay. At main road turn left to signpost indicating pedestrian tunnel to the right. At the entrance to the tunnel an information board gives details about the period George Stephenson spent at a house that once stood there. He was employed at a haulage installation on the large ballast hill which used to occupy the area now used as a car-park by the Cookson lead factory on your right.

The pedestrian and cycle tunnels were created just after the last war to replace a free ferry which crossed the river at this point. The ferry's main function was to give the many thousands of shipyard workers living on either side of the river easy access to their workplaces. These tunnels now seem rather superfluous, since the workforce has declined and the Tyne road tunnel, now carrying the A1, has been built.

Descend to the pedestrian tunnel and walk under the river — expect a spooky atmosphere, since you will probably have the route to yourself! At

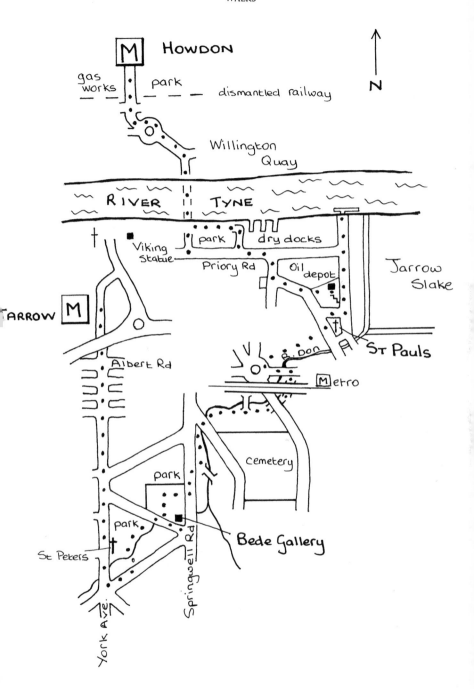

the time of their installation the escalators were claimed to be the highest in Europe, perhaps they still are — certainly the view is impressive whether you are travelling up or down. Going up, you can experience a strange optical illusion: if you lean backwards the escalator appears to be almost vertical.

Leaving the exit, turn back into Riverside Park. The views from here tend to be dominated by the huge bulk of North Sea oil platforms, the building of which has largely replaced that of ships. Walk along the river front to the right. Above you is the monument to Charles Palmer on whose enterprises — mining, shipping, iron manufacture and shipbuilding — Jarrow grew from a village to a town of some 40,000 people. When these industries failed in the 30s, the town sank into poverty. *(See page 35)* Today things aren't so bad, although the town can hardly be described as thriving.

From the end of the park take the lane away from the river; dry docks are on your left. Follow Priory Road to your left as far as the *Duke of Wellington* on the right; there turn left between the oil depots. This unlikely approach will bring you to Jarrow Hall and a complete change of scene.

The Hall (closed Mondays) contains items from the monastery excavations, photographs and reconstructions; art exhibitions are also held. From the hall garden and its herb display, steps lead to a park and picnic area sloping down to the site of the monastery. On your left, beyond the old park wall, was Jarrow Slake — an inland sea a mile wide into which the little River Don discharged next to the monastery.

Over the years the slake has shrunk — first by the formation of Tyne Dock in its eastern half and, more recently, landfill reclamation. Prior to this it was used as a seasoning pond by timber importers; huge baulks of wood floated on the tide — Catherine Cookson enthusiasts will be familiar with the scene for her adventures here are featured in her autobiography, *Our Kate*.

The Slake's removal has changed the site of the monastery from waterside to inland.

Leaving the park to your left, go down steps through the old wall until you reach the Slake Road. This runs below the hall to the river, ending at an old jetty: this is private property but the security gate is likely to be open, so access is at your own risk. There used to be open water along this road; now there is grass and trees. Beyond is the Don, extended to the Tyne by a channel best viewed at high tide. In this deserted area the only sounds you are likely to hear are the calls of oystercatchers and other waterside birds.

In the other direction the road ends at the bridge over the mouth of the Don. This is now barred, though a footpath continues below the monastery to the new bridge. Don't take it; instead leave the road to visit St Pauls church and the ruins of the famous monastery, home of the Venerable Bede. *(See page 28)*

The tall Saxon church is now the chancel, at the west end of which is a narrow early-Norman tower dividing it from the nave. The Norman nave was destroyed in 1786 and rebuilt 80 years later by Gilbert Scott. At the same time the north aisle was added. Foundations of the earlier buildings have been found under the present floor. Amazingly, the dedication stone of 684 survives, as does 'Bede's' ancient chair which actually dates from some years later. One of the windows contains glass from the Saxon period.

The monastery ruins are mainly 11th century with later modifications, though portions of the Saxon building have been found. They are well labelled and displayed with explanatory plans. This was Bede's home from the age of 12 until his death some 50 years later in 735 when he was still working on his history of the English church and its people. His was one of the first accounts to be based on research rather than legend. More about Bede can be found in the Jarrow Hall Museum.

Leaving the churchyard by the main west gate, cross the road and take the ash path opposite which leads up the Don valley; tree planting has made this a pleasant walk. Reaching the big roundabout at the entrance to the vehicle tunnel, take the South Shields road left to a footpath on its right leading under the Metro and the A1 to a further stretch of landscaped riverside. Pass on your right a new laminated timber footbridge and continue up the valley with a large wooded cemetery above you on the left. Reaching the foot of Cemetery Road turn right to another footpath entry beyond both the road and the river.

Continue up the far side of the river to cross the path making for a small bridge. Turn right over grass to Springwell Road to get past engineering works, behind which Monkton Dene flows into the Don. Beyond the white-painted hall on the right, enter Springwell Park. Keep to the high path on the right hand side, leading to the Longmore Fountain which stands on a knoll. Drop down beyond it to Butcher's Bridge Road and turn left over the valley to reach the Bede Gallery, formed within a large air-raid shelter in the corner of the park. The gallery, open each day except Saturday and Monday, concentrates on contemporary art and local history.

Recross valley and enter Monkton Dene Park on the far side of road. Continue through the park, crossing the stream, and exit into York Avenue. Turn right over the bridge and cross the road to look up the next stretch of valley, pleasantly wooded to commemorate the Festival of Britain in 1951. The little valley continues up through Monkton to Leam Lane, but you are already get-ting out of range of the Metro. The mile between here and the town centre is an unexciting street walk and you may weaken and want to catch a bus from this point, just opposite St Peters church — an attractive modern building. Otherwise it is a straight walk along York Avenue and its continuation, Bede Burn Road, to Jarrow station. Bede's Well is away to your left — somewhat inaccessible.

Just beyond the station is Jarrow town centre dominated by the tall spire of Christ Church, which makes an impressive background to the sculpture on the far side of the shopping precinct which commemorates the Viking landing at Jarrow. The nearby town hall is a Victorian building with a large clock projecting over the pavement; its richness is in sharp contrast to the shops opposite.

The South Bank: Hebburn to Gateshead

4 miles

*Forty years ago the land along this riverbank walk would
have been devoted mainly to industrial activity. Today
recreation plays the major role.*

FROM Hebburn Metro station turn north and head down towards the Tyne. Most of Hebburn lies behind you, stretching south east until only Campbell Park separates it from Jarrow. Like most of the towns along the lower valley, it once had extensive mining and ship-building industries: now it is dominated by heavy electrical engineering.

The small area between the Metro and the river is an interesting relic: a few terraces of various periods, some tree-lined, a pair of rather lonely-looking banks, and an impressive church.

Pass to the right of Barclays Bank then turn right at Lyon Street towards St Andrew's United Reformed Church. This is a large lofty church in 13th century Gothic erected in 1872 by the ship-builder Andrew Leslie. Alongside it is an equally massive school, now used as small workshops by the St Andrew's Centre. Turn down Ann Street on the near side of the centre to a grassy area on the site of old ballast hills. To your right Ellison Street leads down to the abandoned terminus of the Low Walker and Wallsend ferries, once much used by riverside workers.

Leave the grassed areas at the far left hand corner to gain the riverside and follow the bank upsteam. Strike up an inclined cycleway into the Hebburn Riverside Park. The path, though kerb-ed, is grown over with grass and follows the upper edges of a large mown area running along the side of new tree plant-ing. Below, the edge of the river is lined with moorings for small craft; on the far, Low Walker, shore are engineering works. There will probably be partially-built oil rigs in view and the river's large floating crane is likely to be moored there.

The bank, however, is truly rural — partly because the railway, now Metro, line cuts it off from the more level ground beyond, where development has been concentrated. Once the river bank accommodated small slipways and the Primrose and Pelaw Main staithes served by wagonways: now the only sounds are bird song. An Off-shore Technology Park is to be built on the site opposite. The walk so far has been southward, heading towards Washington, but after crossing the boundary from South Tyneside to Gates-head the course of the river swings west (and then, at St Anthony's Point, north westerly). The white tower of the Newcastle Civic Centre can be seen in the distance.

Bill Quay occupies a creek-like bulge where a wide stretch of watercourse has eaten into the outside (south) of a sharp bend. A small shipyard occupies this space and a plaque records its ori-gins — Harrison's Yard opened in 1900 in succession to one established prior to 1820 by W. Boutland. Here, tugs and wherries, first in timber and later in metal, and small iron steamers were built — the traditional beginnings of most of the region's shipbuilding com-panies.

Time out at Gateshead Stadium

Keeping to the perimeter of the ship-yard, ahead lies the Albion Inn, one of a few scattered along the shores of the river. The road to Pelaw Station strikes up the hill on your left, past the Cromwell pub to the City Farm if you wish to visit. You will there be able to see another of Gateshead's art works, this time the *Chicken Run* by Andy Frost, a colourful slide in the form of a giant chicken. But to continue the riverside walk turn along Jonadab Road — a high factory wall will be on your right.

Where the wall gives way to alder plantings the river can be recovered along a rough road leading to Heworth Shore. Just about here was the St Anthony's Ferry, a rowing boat which plied, on demand, across to the foot of Pottery Bank opposite. There is now a riverside park on the north bank and the little ferry is no more.

Around about the site of the park, there used to be a station on the old Riverside Branch electric railway, the course of which can be seen running upriver to St Peter's station. Here the track was close to the river and the stone retaining wall and arches which supported it can easily be distinguished.

At Heworth Shore the river edge is blocked by a large paint factory. Take the footpath on the left of its security fence, curving up between it and the back gardens of houses. Ignore a tempting short cut alongside the factory when the security gates at each end are open but follow the track round the playing field to Stoneygate Lane. Turn right to factory entrance and left to supermarket. Follow footpath on right of this down to the old Nest Road leading you past the sites of Nest House and the Felling Staithes to Friar's Goose.

A new railway bridge across the Tyne was planned at this point to bring the main Edinburgh line south from Benton to bypass Newcastle. Parts of the reservation kept clear of development can still be identified in Walker.

Keeping to the right, drop to Friar's Goose Slipway, now used as moorings.

153

Pass to the left of the Riverside Lodge Hotel and climb on to the landscaped Tyne Main spoil heap. On your left is an impressive ruin which could pass, with its five foot thick walls, as that of a small castle; do not be misled: it was an old mine-head.

Nearby is a three-armed signpost. Here you have a choice of path. By taking that to the right the riverside path can be continued along the Salt Meadows for another half mile to South Shore Road. This leads to the Swing bridge but is a fairly busy, unattractive road with little view. More can be seen by keeping to higher ground. Take the path ahead to Tyne Main Road, cross it and climb the grassy hill. To the south you look down upon playing pitches divided by grass-covered hills and terraces, to the right is the Gateshead International Stadium. Across the river opposite you is Byker, the new housing falling away from St Michael's Church spire. On its left can be glimpsed Glasshouse bridge spanning the Ouseburn mouth.

Drop down to the Stadium and circle it to the left. At the far end of the buildings on your side (east) of the enclosure are some steps — take them to get a view into the arena — now the venue for major international athletics meetings. There will probably be figures training on the track. From the main entrance continue across the car park to right side of pub. Cross Neilson Road and turn left to dual carriageway. Cross this by the pedestrian bridge a short distance to right. Continue along far side of dual carriageway to turn left before car showroom (James Road) to reach Gateshead Stadium Metro station.

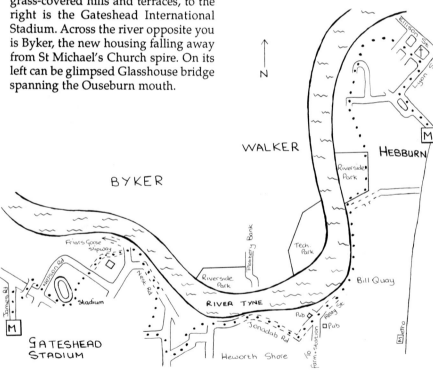

154

COOKSON COUNTRY IS LONG SANDY BEACHES AND ROLLING SURF, RUGGED
    CLIFFS WITH SECRETIVE CAVES WHERE CORMORANTS, KITTIWAKES AND
    HERRING GULLS FLY.

COOKSON COUNTRY IS FAIRGROUND AND FOUNTAINS, FISHING AND BOATING,
    SAILING AND SURFING, SAND CASTLES, DECK-CHAIRS, ICE CREAM, CANDY
    FLOSS AND A PLODGE IN THE SEA.

COOKSON COUNTRY IS ROMAN LEGIONS, VIKINGS AND THE MONKS OF ST. BEDE,
    BYGONE SHIPS AND MODERN SHIPS AND LIFEBOAT PIONEERS, IT'S MARKET
    DAYS AND SHOPPING, BRIGHT LIGHTS AND WINING, DINING AND DANCING.

COOKSON COUNTRY IS THE FIFTEEN STREETS, THE GAMBLING MAN, OUR KATE
    AND SO MUCH MORE.

Further information available from Press & Promotions Office, South Tyneside MBC,
Town Hall, Westoe Road, South Shields NE33 2RL. Tel. (091) 427 1717.

Catherine Cookson
COUNTRY

That's South Tyneside!

JUST 15 MINUTES FROM THE NATIONAL GARDEN FESTIVAL

Useful information

NEWCASTLE

BUILDINGS
Bessie Surtees House, Sandhill
Central Metro and BR station
Blackfriars Centre, Blackfriars
St James Metro station
Castle Keep, Saint Nicholas Street
Central Metro and BR station
City Walls, Bath Lane/Stowell Street/Friars Street area and Broad Chare
St James Metro station
Grey's Monument, Grey Street
Monument Metro
Hadrian's Wall, The Roman Way, Denton
Bus nos. 31, 33 & 38
Keelmen's Hospital, City Road
Central Metro and BR station
St Andrew's Church, Darn Crook
St James Metro
St Nicholas' Cathedral, Mosley Street
Central Metro and BR station
MUSEUMS
Museum of Antiquities, Newcastle University
Haymarket Metro
Hancock Museum, Barras Bridge
Haymarket Metro
Hatton Gallery, The Quadrangle, Newcastle University
Haymarket Metro
John George Joicey Museum, City Road
Manors BR station
Worswick Street bus station
Laing Art Gallery, Higham Place
Monument Metro
Military Vehicle Museum, Exhibition Park
Jesmond Metro
Newburn Hall Motor Museum, Townfield Gardens
Bus nos. 21, 22, 23, 49, 54, 71
Science & Engineering Museum, Blandford Square, Central Metro & BR station
Side Gallery, The Side
Centrol Metro & BR station/Manors BR station
Trinity Maritime Centre, Broad Chare, Quayside
Central Metro and BR station

MARKETS
Armstrong Bridge, Jesmond Dene
West Jesmond Metro
Bigg Market
Monument Metro
Grainger Market, Grainger Street
Monument Metro
Green Market, Clayton Street
Monument
Guildhall, Quayside
Central Metro and BR station
Quayside
Central Metro and BR station
PARKS
Armstrong Park, Heaton
Chillingham Road/West Jesmond Metros
Exhibition Park
Haymarket Metro
Heaton Park
Chillingham Road/West Jesmond Metros
Jesmond Dene
West Jesmond Metro
Leazes Park, Barrack Road
St James Metro
Nuns Moor Park
Bus nos. 32, 32A, 36
Town Moor
Bus nos. 17, 47, 48, 76E, 77E, 78E, X71, X73, X77, X87, X88, V87
SPORTING VENUES, ETC.
Brough Park, Brough Park, Byker
Byker Metro interchange. Bus nos. 21, 71
Eldon Square Recreation Centre
Monument Metro
Gosforth Park Racecourse, Wideopen, Gosforth
Palmesville/Gosforth Metro . Bus nos. 363, X25, X26
St James Park, Newcastle
St James Metro
THEATRES
City Hall, Northumberland Road
Haymarket Metro
Playhouse, Barras Bridge
Haymarket Metro
Peoples Theatre , Stephenson Road
Jesmond Metro
Live Theatre, 27 Broad Chare, Quayside
Central Metro and BR station

Theatre Royal, Grey Street
Monument Metro
Tyne Theatre and Opera House, Westgate Road
Central Metro and BR station

GATESHEAD

BUILDINGS
Gibside Chapel, Burnopfield
Blaydon BR station. Bus no. 715
Winlaton Cottage Forge, Church Street, Winlaton
Blaydon BR station. Winlaton bus station, bus nos.
639, 640, 641, 642, 648, 649, M4, M5, M7, M9
MUSEUMS/PRESERVED RAILWAYS
Shipley Art Gallery, Prince Consort Rd, Gateshead
Gateshead Metro station. Bus nos. 53, 54
Tanfield Railway, Sunniside, Gateshead
Central Metro and BR station.Bus nos. X30, 644, M3,
705, 06, 07, 08, 771, X11, X36
Causey Arch, between Sunniside and Stanley
Central Metro and BR station. Bus no. X30
PARKS
Saltwell Park, Gateshead
Gateshead Stadium Metro. Bus nos. 53, 54, 24, 26, 28,
231, 709,722, 723, 728, 735, OK, LF
Thornley Wood/Winlaton Mill
Blaydon BR station.Bus nos. 639, 640, 641, 642,648,
649, M4, M5, M7, M9
SPORTING VENUES, ETC.
International Stadium, Neilson Road, Gateshead
Gateshead Stadium Metro .Bus nos. 93, 93A, 94, 94A
Leisure Centre, Alexandra Road, Gateshead
Gateshead Stadium Metro.Bus nos. 61, 62
THEATRES
Caedmon Hall, Central Library, Prince Consort
Road, Gateshead
Gateshead Stadium Metro.Bus nos. 53, 54, 61, 62, 88,
89, 90, M31, M33
MARKETS
Gateshead Market
Gateshead Metro Interchange

NORTH TYNESIDE

BUILDINGS
Hadrian's Wall, Richardson Dees Park, Kings Road,
Wallsend
Wallsend Metro and bus interchange.Bus nos. 303,
304, 307, 313, 314, 319, 320, 321, 330, 331, 340, 341

Lord Collingwood Monument, Tynemouth
Tynemouth Metro.Bus nos. 300, 301, 315, 316, 325,
326, 332, 333, 342
Tynemouth Castle and Priory, Tynemouth
Tynemouth Metro.Bus nos. 306, 332, 333
St Mary's Lighthouse, Trinity Road, Whitley Bay
West Monkseaton Metro.Bus nos. 308, 310, 317, 332,
333, X16, W8
Stephenson's 'Dial' Cottage, Great Lime Road,
Killingworth
Palmersville Metro.Bus nos. 313, 314, 342, 343, 344,
346, 355, M55
MARKETS
North Shields Fish Market Fish Quay, North Shields
North Shields Metro.Bus nos. 302, 332, 333
Tynemouth Station, Tynemouth
Tynemouth Metro.Bus nos. 300, 301, 315, 316, 325,
326, 332, 333, 342
Spanish City, Whitley Bay
Whitley Bay Metro.Bus nos. 300, 301, 307, 308, 309,
310, 315, 316, 317, 325, 326, 332, 333, 346, X16, W3, W8
Wallsend Indoor Market, Carville Road, Wallsend
Wallsend Metro interchange.Bus nos. 3, 20, 21, 34,
49, 71, 301, 302, 303, 307, 323, 324
MUSEUMS
Holly House Gallery, 14 Front Street, Tynemouth
Tynemouth Metro.Bus nos. 306, 332, 333
Buddle Arts Centre, 258b Station Road, Wallsend
Wallsend Metro interchange.Bus nos. 303, 304, 307,
313, 314, 319, 320, 321, 330, 331, 340, 341
Wallsend Heritage Centre, Station Road, Wallsend
Wallsend Metro interchange.Bus nos. 34, 35, 35A
Tynemouth Volunteer Life Brigade Collection, Brigade Cottage, Spanish Battery, Tynemouth
Tynemouth Metro.Bus nos. 306, 332, 222
Stephenson Railway Museum, Middle Engine Lane,
North Shields
Percy Main Metro.Bus nos. 300, 307
PARKS
Churchill Park, opposite Souter Park, Whitley Bay
Monkseaton Metro.Bus nos. 325, 326, 359, 442, 810,
811, W4
Northumberland Park, Tynemouth
Tynemouth Metro.Bus nos. 97, 306, 310, N
Richardson Dees Park, Kings Road, Wallsend
Wallsend Metro interchange.Bus nos. 304, 307
Tynemouth Park, Grand Parade, Tynemouth
Tynemouth Metro.Bus nos. 301, 315, 316, 325, 326,
332, 333

Marden Park, Whitley Bay
Whitley Bay.Bus nos. 344, 442, 810, 811
SPORTING VENUES, ETC
Whitley Bay Leisure Pool, The Links, Whitley Bay
Whitley Bay/Monkseaton Metros.Bus nos. 308, 310,
317, 332, 333, X16, W3, W8
Whitley Bay Ice Rink and Ten Pin Bowling Centre,
Hillheads Road, Whitley Bay
Monkseaton/Whitley Bay Metros.Bus nos. 308, 317,
343, 344, 442, 810, 811
Spanish City, Whitley Bay
Whitley Bay Metro.Bus nos. 300, 301, 307, 308, 309,
310, 315, 316, 317, 325, 326, 332, 333, 346, X16, W3, W8
THEATRES
Buddle Art Centre, Station Road, Wallsend
Wallsend Metro.Bus nos. 303, 304, 307, 313, 314, 319,
320, 321, 330, 340, 341
Playhouse, Marine Avenue, Whitley Bay
W.Bay/Monkseaton Metro.Bus nos. 46, 348, 810, 811

SOUTH TYNESIDE

BUILDINGS
St Paul's Church, Church Bank, Jarrow
Jarrow/Bede Metro.Bus nos. 525, 526, 527
Old Town Hall, Market Place, South Shields
Municipal Buildings, Fowler Street, South Shields
South Shields Metro.Bus nos. 1, 2, 6, 7, 8, 13, 14, 50,
535, 536, E2, X2
MARKETS
South Shields, Market Place
South Shields Metro.Bus nos 1, 2, 6, 7, 8, 13, 14, 50,
535, 536, E2, X2
MUSEUMS
Bede Gallery, Springwell Park, Butchers Bridge
Road, Jarrow
Jarrow/Bede Metro.Bus no. 521
Bede Monastery Museum, Jarrow Hall, Church
Bank, Jarrow
Jarrow/Bede Metro.Bus nos. 525, 526, 527
Arbeia Roman Fort and Museum, Baring Street,
South Shields
South Shields Metro.Bus no. 501
South Shields Museum, Ocean Road, South Shields
South Shields Metro.Bus nos. 10, 11, 501, E1
PARKS
Bents Park, Sea Road, South Shields
South Shields Metro.Bus nos. 10, 11, E1, 13, 14
Carr Ellison Park, Hebburn

Hebburn Metro.Bus nos. 521, 532, 538, 544
Monkton Dene Park, York Avenue, Monkton
Hebburn Metro.Bus nos. 539, 544
North Marine Park, Harbour Drive, South Shields
South Shields Metro.Bus nos. 10, 11, E1, 501
South Shields Marine Park, Sea Road, South Shields
South Shields Metro.Bus nos. 10, 11, E1, 13, 14, 501
SPORTS VENUES
Gypsies' Green Sports Stadium, Broadway, South
Shields
South Shields Metro.Bus nos. E1, 13, 14
Temple Park Leisure Pool, John Reid Road, South
Shields
Tyne Dock Metro.Bus nos. 1, 2, 3, 4, 10, 11, 16, 17, 531,
533, 551, 553, 554, X2
Marsden Rock and Grotto
Tyne Dock Metro.Bus no. E1
THEATRES
Pier Pavilion Theatre, Pier Parade, South Shields
South Shields Metro.Bus nos. 10, 11, E1

SUNDERLAND

BUILDINGS
Hylton Castle Estate
Bus nos. 131, 135, 136, 186, X4
Penshaw Monument, Penshaw
Bus nos. 638, 775, 777, 778, X6
St Peter's Church, Saint Peter's Way
Central BR Station
Bus no. E1
Washington Old Hall, The Avenue, Washington
(No station)
Bus nos. 171, 178, 185, 291
MUSEUMS
Grindon Museum, Grindon Lane
(No station)
Bus nos. 15, 16, 18, 19
Monkwearmouth Station Museum, North Bridge
Street
Central BR Station
Bus nos. 4, 5, 6, 7, 17, 19, 23, 24, 25, 27, 28, 29, 100, 104,
107, 118, 119, 130, 131, 164, 185, 186, 188, 310, 319, 535,
536, 587, 538, X2, X4, X86, X88, X96, E1, E2, E3
North East Aircraft Museum, Washington Road
Bus nos. 185, 187, 188, 551, X88
Ryhope Engines Museum
Seaham BR Station
Bus nos. 137, X96

Sunderland Museum and Art Gallery, Borough Road
Central BR Station
Bus nos. 139, 140
Washington 'F' Pit Industrial Museum, Albany Way, District 2, Washington
Bus nos. 177, 178, 291, 292, Or, Gr, Tr
PARKS
Barnes Park
Bus nos. 6, 16, 18, 19
Mowbray Park, Burdon Road
Central BR Station)
Bus nos. 139, 140, 18, 118, 134
Princess Anne Park, Washington
Bus nos. 165, X5, X6, X7, X93, X94, 638, 776
Roker Park, Roker Park Road
Seaburn BR Station
Bus nos. 18, 19, 118, 119, X2, E1, E3
Sir James Steel Park, Washington
Bus nos. 294, 638, 731, 777
Silksworth Complex, Sunderland

Bus nos. X13, 31, 32, 133
SPORTS VENUES
Crowtree Leisure Centre, Crowtree Road
Central BR Station
Central Bus Station
Northumbria Centre, Stephenson Industrial Estate, Washington
Bus nos. 291, 292, 298, 299
Roker Park
Seaburn BR Station
Bus nos. 18, 19, 118, 119, X2, E1, E3
Washington Waterfowl Park, Dist. 15, Washington
Bus nos. 186, X4, X6, X86, X95

COUNTY DURHAM

Beamish Open Air Museum, Nr. Chester-le-Street, Co. Durham
(No trains, no buses – nearest is X30 along Causey Road, or 22, 28, 29, M29, all terminate at The Square, Kibblesworth.

A comprehensive information pack, *Out and About in Tyne and Wear*, published by Tyne & Wear PTE, is available from local travel centres — *see page 55*

Gibside Chapel and Grounds, Rowlands Gill

THE NATIONAL TRUST NORTHUMBRIA

An outstanding example of Palladian architecture, this Georgian Chapel stands at one end of the Great Walk of Turkey Oaks leading to the monument of British Liberty. Set in an 18th century landscaped park. Formerly home of the Bowes Lyon family.

Tel: Consett (0207) 542255

Open: 1 April - 31 Oct.except Mon. (open Bank Holiday Mon.) 11 - 5. Last admission 4.30. **Admission:** Adults £1.50. **Location:** 6m SW of Gateshead. **Facilities:** Shop, tea room, picnic area, circular walks.

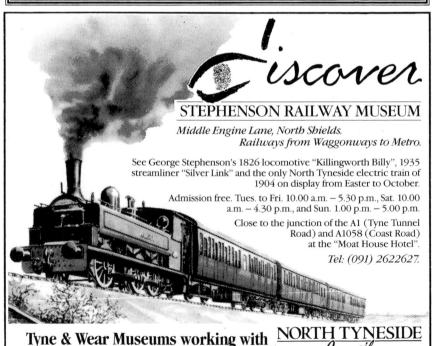